BEYOND LIMITS - MANIFESTING AND UNLEASHING YOUR DREAM CAREER

STEPHANIE MAHALIA FLETCHER-LARTEY

BEYOND LIMITS - MANIFESTING AND UNLEASHING YOUR DREAM CAREER

Title Page

Beyond Limits: Manifesting and Unleashing Your Dream Career.

A Comprehensive Career Planning Resource Guide

Foreword by Kelly Markey

Copyright @ Stephanie Mahalia Fletcher-Lartey

ISBN: 9780645484656

Suggested Citation: Fletcher-Lartey, Stephanie Mahalia. *Beyond Limits: Manifesting and Unleashing Your Dream Career. A Comprehensive Career Planning Resource Guide.* Australia: Stephanie Fletcher-Lartey, 2025.

Copyright and Professional Disclaimer

Copyright 2025 © Stephanie M. Fletcher-Lartey

All rights reserved.

ISBN: 9780645484656.

No portion of this book may be reproduced in any form without written permission from the author, except as permitted by Australian and international copyright law, **and as specifically outlined below.**

Limited Permission for Educational and Personal Use:

The templates, worksheets, and exercises included within this publication may be reproduced or printed solely for the purchaser's personal use or for formal, non-commercial educational and classroom purposes, provided that the copyright notice remains intact on all copies. No other portion of the text may be reproduced or transmitted without explicit written permission.

Professional Disclaimer:

This publication is designed to provide accurate and authoritative professional development and career coaching information. The author, Dr. Stephanie M. Fletcher-Lartey, is a Certified Life and Career Coach with the requisite qualifications to cover the subject matter herein.

However, this book does not guarantee specific results, as **success and transformation are based solely on the reader's personal efforts, commitment, and application of the strategies.**

This material is sold with the understanding that neither the author nor the publisher is engaged in rendering legal, financial, medical, or other specialised professional services. While the author and publisher have used their best efforts in preparing this book, they make no representations or warranties with respect to the accuracy or **completeness** of the contents of this book and specifically disclaim any implied warranties of merchantability or fitness for a particular purpose.

The advice and strategies contained herein may not be suitable for your specific situation. You should consult with an appropriate professional when required. Neither the publisher nor the author shall be liable for any loss of profit or any other commercial damages, including but not limited to special, incidental, consequential, or other damages arising from the use of this material.

Image and Generative AI Disclosure:

All original images and illustrations used within the text of this book were created by the author, Dr. Stephanie M. Fletcher-Lartey, with the assistance of the Gemini 2.5 Flash generative AI and ChatGPT (GPT-5) models. This use is formally cited as:

Google. (2024). *Gemini 2.5 Flash* [Generative AI model] and OpenAI. (2025). ChatGPT (GPT-5) [Large language model]. https://chat.openai.com/

Book Cover designed by Stephanie M. Fletcher-Lartey

Published in Australia.

CONTENTS

Foreword — xi
Preface — xiii
About The Author — xvii
Introduction — xxi

SECTION ONE — 1

  1 Designing a Dream for Your Career — 2
  2 Overcoming Fears and Blockers to Career — 11
  3 Understanding Barriers — 22
  4 Cultivating a Resilience Mindset — 26

SECTION TWO — 30

Section 2: Overview of Career Action Planning — 31

  5 Understanding Career Planning — 33
  6 Step 1: Skills Assessment — 37
  7 Steps 2-3: Career Goal Setting and Researching — 45
  8 Step 4: Understanding Skills Gaps — 53
  9 Step 5: Leveraging Transferable Skills — 61
  10 Step 6: Creating a Comprehensive Career Plan — 78
  11 Step 7: Monitoring and Adjusting Your Plan — 87
  12 Continuous Learning and Professional Relationships — 91

SECTION THREE — 99

  13 Navigating the Global Employment Maze — 100
  14 The Entrepreneurial Mindset: — 109
  15 Chapter 15: Building Your Business: — 113

Epilogue — 118

Endorsements	121
Other Books by Stephanie Fletcher-Lartey	124
APPENDICES	129
Appendix 1: Career Dream Blueprint: A Worksheet	130
Appendix 2: The Growth & Resilience Toolkit	138
Appendix 3: Skills Development & Growth Plan	141
Appendix 4: Personal Brand Statement Worksheet	149
Appendix 5: Résumé & Cover Letter Checklist	150
Appendix 6: LinkedIn Profile Optimising Checklist	151
Appendix 7: Comprehensive Career Action Plan	152
Appendix 8: Continuous Learning and Relationships	157
Bibliography	160
Index	162

Foreword

"For I know the plans I have for you," declares the Lord, "plans to prosper you and not to harm you, plans to give you hope and a future." — Jeremiah 29:11

It is with deep honour and joy that I pen this foreword for *Beyond Limits: Manifesting and Unleashing Your Dream Career* by Dr. Stephanie Mahalia Fletcher-Lartey. From the very first time I met Dr. Stephanie; our connection was natural and effortless—like ducks to water. There was an instant recognition of shared values, vision, and a mutual desire to bring light, hope, and transformation into the world.

Our paths intertwined meaningfully when Dr. Stephanie co-authored the anthology *Echoes of Humanity*, which I had the privilege to publish through Markey Writing Academy. In that book, she contributed her voice to a chorus of powerful testimonies, reflections, and stories that have since touched hearts globally. That collaboration revealed not only her brilliance as a writer but also her unwavering commitment to lifting others through words, wisdom, and lived experience. It gives me even greater delight now to see her step boldly into authorship once again, this time with a resource guide that equips individuals to pursue careers with purpose, resilience, and determination.

When I look back at my own journey, I see a path marked by both trials and triumphs. There were seasons of hardship where the weight of betrayal, loss, and even illness felt overwhelming. There were also seasons of victory, where hope shone through the darkness and reminded me that no circumstance has the final word over our destiny. Through it all, I discovered that purpose often emerges in the midst of pain, and that resilience, courage, and vision can unlock doors that once seemed permanently shut.

It is from this perspective that I recommend *Beyond Limits*. This is not just another career guide—it is a call to action, a road map, and a beacon of encouragement for all who long to create a brighter, more purposeful future. Dr. Stephanie Mahalia Fletcher-Lartey has crafted a resource that speaks across cultures, across generations, and across circumstances. It acknowledges the challenges faced by many around the world, especially those in environments where opportunity is scarce, while at the same time pointing toward possibility, strategy, and hope.

The beauty of this book lies in its balance. On one hand, it is practical: full of insights, steps, and strategies that readers can apply to their own journey. On the other hand, it is deeply inspiring, reminding us that careers are not just about survival or titles but about building lives of meaning and impact. Dr. Fletcher-Lartey empowers readers to dream bigger, to plan with intention, and to persist with confidence even when the road feels uncertain.

As an Ambassador of Hope, I have seen how powerful it is when people are given not only encouragement but also tools to transform their lives. Hope alone can lift the human spirit, but when paired with actionable strategies, it becomes unstoppable. That is exactly what *Beyond Limits* offers—both the spark to believe and the guidance to achieve. It is a book that does not merely sit on a shelf but walks alongside its readers, urging them to step forward with courage.

I am deeply honoured to amplify this message and to join in taking the hope contained within these pages to people everywhere. To the graduate wondering what comes next, to the professional searching for a renewed sense of direction, to the dreamer daring to believe in something more—this book offers a lifeline. It carries the promise of brighter opportunities and the assurance that no dream is too distant when you dare to go beyond limits.

As you journey through these pages, I invite you to read with both your heart and your mind open. Let the words challenge you, encourage you, and equip you. Allow yourself to envision not just a career but a life that reflects your deepest values and aspirations. The path may not always be easy, but with the guidance provided here, you will find yourself better prepared to walk it with confidence and hope.

In today's rapidly changing world, career success is not simply about securing employment; it is about cultivating resilience, adaptability, and self-belief. Dr. Stephanie Mahalia Fletcher–Lartey has carefully crafted a resource that combines practical tools with deep insights. Whether you are navigating the uncertainties of the global job market, striving to stand out in a competitive environment, or searching for meaning in your professional life, this book provides the clarity and confidence you need to move forward. It is my privilege to commend this book to you. May it inspire you, guide you, and propel you toward the limitless possibilities that await.

Kelly Markey
Award-Winning & Best-Selling Author
CEO of Markey Writing Academy
Founder & Global Director of Beacon of Hope Mission
Ambassador of Hope

Preface

Beyond Boundaries

Welcome to a resource designed not just to guide your career, but to transform your professional life. As a Public Health Epidemiologist who has worked extensively across global boundaries, I have been privileged to witness first-hand the incredible resilience and untapped potential within professionals everywhere. However, I have also seen the common struggles: the lack of clarity on career direction, the difficulty in navigating multicultural job markets, and the challenge of aligning one's professional life with a deeper sense of purpose.

Beyond Limits: *Manifesting and Unleashing Your Dream Career*, A Comprehensive Career Planning Resource Guide, is a culmination of years of professional experience, research, and insights gathered from coaching hundreds of professionals worldwide. It is built on the belief that your career should be a calling—a purposeful, fulfilling journey that leverages your unique gifts and talents.

Most people already know, at a fundamental level, what steps will set them on the path to career success. Yet, many hesitate to embrace this truth because it demands hard work, collaboration, understanding corporate objectives, and, crucially, confronting personal and professional challenges. This book is written for those who are ready to move beyond hesitation and transform their aspirations into achievements. As someone who has navigated the volatile and rewarding path of career development and several pivotal transitions, my journey stands as testament to these truths. Through my own experiences and the stories of hundreds of professionals I have mentored, it became undeniably clear that sharing this structured knowledge—the how and the why—could empower a new generation of leaders.

My commitment to this mission led to the creation of 'My Career My Calling,' initially as a radio programme on Down Under Radio, and later as an ongoing podcast and professional training platform to support professionals (initially focused on highly skilled migrants in navigating multicultural job markets), to gain clarity and thrive in the marketplace.

Driven by a passion to connect and empower public health professionals globally, I also founded the Global Public Health Connect Network (GPHCoN)—a platform providing mentorship, collaboration, and skill enhancement, particularly for those in developing and underdeveloped countries.

The Power of Self-Reflection

Your journey starts with self-discovery. By taking an honest look at who you are, what you value, and what you're capable of, you can make intentional career choices that lead to professional and personal fulfilment. Start by reflecting on your strengths, weaknesses, and aspirations. Consider your past experiences to identify patterns of success and struggle. It's also crucial to recognise your core values, as these guide your decisions and ensure your career aligns with your personal ethics. Let these values guide your vision and long-term goals.

You can utilise several tools to aid this self-assessment:

- **SWOT analysis** to evaluate your strengths, weaknesses, opportunities, and threats.
- **Skill inventories** to identify areas for improvement.
- **Personality assessments** to discover suitable work roles and develop your natural strengths.

Navigating Challenges and Embracing Change

Every journey has its obstacles. These can be internal, like self-doubt, or external, such as systemic challenges. However, these barriers are not immovable. Just as the world is in a state of constant change—with rapid technological advancements like automation and AI reshaping traditional roles—you, too, must be ready to adapt. Resilience and adaptability are essential for long-term success. Resilience allows you to bounce back from setbacks, while adaptability enables you to navigate new situations with flexibility. This requires a growth mindset, where you see challenges as opportunities to learn and grow, not as insurmountable obstacles.

The ability to embrace change and overcome limiting beliefs is powered by a few key strategies:

- Embracing a growth mindset by viewing challenges as opportunities.
- Focusing on your vision to fuel your actions.
- Viewing failure as a stepping stone rather than a setback.
- Utilising transferable skills like problem-solving, critical thinking, and communication, which are valuable in any industry. By embracing change and staying committed to growth, you can transform challenges into opportunities and achieve sustained success.

In these pages, I invite you to join a movement of intentional growth. We will go beyond traditional career advice to focus on the inner work—the clarity, resilience, and vision required for sustained success and lasting fulfilment. This book serves as the culmination of these efforts, offering a structured guide that reflects both my professional wisdom and my coaching insights. The principles shared here are universally applicable, but they are framed with the insight gained from working with diverse professionals in complex, dynamic global environments. I aim to empower you with actionable steps and mindset strategies that have proven effective in real-world scenarios. Ultimately, your career potential is the unique combination of your strengths, talents, skills, and passions. This book is your invitation to cultivate the self-awareness, the strategic planning, and the commitment required to go beyond boundaries and achieve your highest potential.

About The Author

Dr. Stephanie Fletcher-Lartey is a multi-talented professional, a true testament to the power of continuous learning, resilience, and vision-driven living, demonstrating how to deploy all innate gifts and talents to their fullest potential. While she has spent nearly three decades building a formidable career in public health, her extensive life's work, reach and impact, demonstrates that her greatest passion is helping others recognise and unleash their own potential.

The Foundation: From Grassroots to Global Health Impact

Dr. Stephanie's professional journey began humbly yet resolutely in 1997 as a Public Health Inspector (PHI) in Jamaica. For over a decade and a half, she mastered the intricacies of environmental health—from outbreak investigation and risk assessments to community-based health promotion. This time at the grassroots level instilled a robust, practical understanding of public health principles.

Driven by a thirst for broader impact, she fortified her career by earning a Master of Public Health and later a Doctor of Philosophy (Ph.D.) in Infectious Disease Epidemiology. These academic achievements paved the way for senior leadership roles on the world stage. As a professional researcher, epidemiologist, and evaluator, her journey features over 67 publications (profiled on Google Scholar). This extensive body of work is a testament to the core strengths she brings to all her roles: analytical rigour, critical thinking, and meticulous attention to detail. These qualities are the guarantee of success for her clients, informing the structured, evidence-based approach she brings to her writing, coaching, and mentoring. Her expertise as a public health epidemiologist was honed while serving diverse communities in Australia and on the global level, where she provided critical policy advice, notably leading the Caribbean COVID-19 response and contributing to WHO's initiatives in the Pacific.

Her dedication to translating research into practice is exemplified by her most recent role as a Senior Research and Evaluation Manager, where she focused on building organisational capacity and consistently mentoring the next generation of public health professionals.

The Multi-Talented Professional

Dr. Stephanie's passion for transformation extends far beyond her formal titles. She is a multi-gifted individual who intentionally utilises her diverse talents to create value:

- **The Author & Thought Leader:** Dr. Stephanie is a committed author and co-author, using her writing to formalise and share her expertise. Her published works include:
    - *The Professional Believer's Guide: Principles to Help Christian Believers Thrive In the Marketplace* (her first book).
    - *The Practice of Journaling Prayer, Testimony, and Gratitude* (including the expanded Kindle edition).
    - Co-author of the anthology, "*Echoes of Humanity: Exploring Human Wonders Through the Pages of: Lessons, Affliction, Triumph, Victory and Brilliance*" (with Kelly Markey).

    She also had the privilege of writing the foreword for Kelly Markey's book, "*Contentment Unravelled,*" inviting readers to explore the many dimensions of contentment through personal encounters and challenges.

- **The Coach & Mentor:** Her commitment to empowering others formalised during the launch of her first book, where the overwhelming response from readers highlighted a significant need for formal coaching and mentorship to live purpose-driven careers. This led her to initially run free workshops for communities to develop purpose-driven career goals setting, which quickly scaled to supporting hundreds of people worldwide and collaborating with other change-makers. Leveraging this extensive experience, she subsequently trained as a professional mentor and became a certified Transformation Coach and Career Reignite Specialist. She utilises performance and evocative coaching to help clients overcome limiting beliefs and manifest their ideal careers.
- **The Creative Artist & Media Producer:** Dr. Stephanie expresses her creativity not only as an actress but also as a singer and songwriter of published songs. She is a committed media producer, creating videos, podcasts, and educational content on her My Career My Calling YouTube platform. Her impact in this space was nominated when her podcast was selected as a Finalist for the Christian Podcast of The Year by Kingdom Women Entrepreneurs Australia.
- **The Advocate & Community Leader:** Recognising the systemic challenges faced by others, she is deeply involved in professional and community leadership. She has served the Jamaican diaspora in Australia and, more broadly, the Asia and the Pacific region through the Global Jamaica Diaspora Council. Her dedicated work as a community champion and a faith-based leader ensures her coaching and mentoring are informed by the comprehensive professional and career development needs across a diverse cross-section of the population. She also developed "My Career My Calling," which began as a radio programme on Down Under Radio and has since expanded into workshops and a dedicated podcast.
- **The Network Founder:** Driven by the overwhelming need for global connection, she recently founded the Global Public Health Connect Network (GPHCoN)—a platform dedicated to bridging gaps and providing mentorship and collaboration opportunities to public health professionals worldwide.

Through this book, Dr. Stephanie draws on her vast experience—from environmental health experiences in Jamaica to policy advice at the global level, and from her stage presence, research rigour, and coaching insights—to empower you to thrive, wherever you are.

INTRODUCTION

Navigating Your Career Journey with Clarity and Purpose

Career progression and growth are natural processes because they align with the human desire for self-improvement, achievement, and fulfilment. As individuals gain experience, develop new skills, and take on greater responsibilities, they naturally seek opportunities to advance in their careers. This progression is not only a reflection of personal ambition but also a response to the evolving demands of the workplace and the broader economy.

Many individuals face significant challenges in their career journeys. These challenges can range from feeling a lack of direction or clarity to experiencing a sense of being stuck with stalled career growth. Many also struggle with the fear of the unknown when contemplating a career change, and the frustration of invisible barriers that hinder advancement. Other common issues include a lack of motivation, underutilised skills, and an inability to overcome self-limiting beliefs that create blockages. These obstacles often lead to dissatisfaction, missed opportunities, and a feeling of being unfulfilled in one's professional life.

These issues are a reflection of interruption or stagnation in the natural career progression process. When this happens, it can have several negative impacts on both personal and professional development:

1. **Personal Development**: Stagnation in career growth can lead to a lack of motivation and engagement. Individuals may feel unchallenged and unfulfilled, which can result in decreased job satisfaction and overall well-being. This lack of fulfilment can spill over into other areas of life, affecting personal relationships and mental health.

2. **Professional Development**: Without opportunities for growth, individuals may find their skills becoming outdated. This can hinder their ability to perform effectively in their current

roles and reduce their competitiveness in the job market. Additionally, the lack of new challenges and learning opportunities can stifle creativity and innovation.

3. **Impact on the Organisation:** When employees experience stagnation, it can lead to decreased productivity and morale. Disengaged employees are less likely to contribute to the organisation's goals and may even become a source of negativity within the workplace. High turnover rates can also result from a lack of career progression opportunities, leading to increased recruitment and training costs for the organisation.

Career progression and growth are essential for maintaining motivation, engagement, and a sense of purpose. When these processes are disrupted, it can have far-reaching consequences for both individuals and the organisations they work for.

The Value of a Career Action Plan

A well-structured career action plan is a valuable tool that can help you navigate and overcome these struggles. A career action plan is a strategic tool that helps individuals navigate their career paths with clarity and purpose. It supports a culture of continuous learning and development that can help professionals achieve their full potential and drive long-term success in their career. It provides a road map to help individuals proactively manage their careers and make informed decisions. It can address the issues of stagnation and lack of growth through:

1. **Goal Setting**: A career action plan encourages individuals to set clear, achievable career goals. This provides direction and motivation, helping to overcome feelings of being stuck or unfulfilled.
2. **Skill Development**: By identifying the skills needed to achieve their goals, individuals can focus on continuous learning and development. This ensures their skills remain relevant and competitive in the job market.
3. **Action Steps**: A career action plan outlines specific actions to take towards career goals. This helps individuals stay proactive and engaged, reducing the risk of stagnation.
4. **Self-Assessment**: Regular self-assessment and reflection are integral to a career action plan. This helps individuals recognise their strengths and areas for improvement, fostering personal and professional growth.
5. **Accountability**: A career action plan provides a framework for tracking progress and holding oneself accountable. This can lead to increased motivation and a sense of accomplishment.
6. **Adaptability**: A career action plan is a dynamic tool that can be adjusted as circumstances change. This flexibility helps individuals navigate career transitions and overcome obstacles more effectively.

By addressing these key areas, a career action plan can help individuals overcome the challenges of career stagnation, leading to greater satisfaction and success in their professional lives. This, in turn, benefits the organisations they work for by fostering a motivated, skilled, and engaged workforce.

On an individual level, a career action plan enhances your confidence, and increases your chances of success by helping you to:

- **Gain Perspective**: Assess where you are and where you want to be, identifying resources and gaps.
- **Stay Focused**: Align your interests, skills, and experiences with your goals to remain on track and enhance your candidacy for desired roles.
- **Set Clear Goals**: Establish specific, measurable, achievable, relevant, and time-bound (SMART) goals to drive your career forward.
- **Develop Strategies**: Outline actionable steps to achieve your career objectives, creating a clear path to success.
- **Embrace Change**: Adopt a flexible mindset that enables you to adapt to new circumstances and opportunities.
- **Maintain Motivation**: Provide a sense of purpose and accomplishment, driving you forward even in the face of challenges.
- **Cultivate Continuous Growth**: Adopt a mindset that emphasises lifelong learning, skill development, and adaptability.

Debunking Common Myths about Career Planning

It is important to address and dismantle common misconceptions about career planning. By challenging these myths, you can adopt a more realistic, adaptable, and empowering approach to your professional journey. Understanding that many common beliefs about career planning are not necessarily true, helps to set the stage for a more informed, flexible, and successful career development process.

It's easy to fall into the trap of believing common myths about career planning, which can often lead to frustration and missed opportunities. This chapter aims to debunk those misconceptions and empower you with a more realistic perspective. A clear understanding of these myths and the realities of career planning is essential for making informed decisions and achieving success.

Myth 1: "You Need to Have Your Entire Career Mapped Out."

- **The Myth:** This widespread belief suggests that you must have a clear, detailed plan for your entire career from the outset, with no room for deviation. It assumes that careers are linear and predictable.
- **The Reality**: Career paths are rarely linear. They often evolve over time due to various factors, including new opportunities, changing interests, and shifts in the job market. It is not necessary to have every detail figured out from the start, and, in fact, it is beneficial to **allow for flexibility and adapt as needed**. Many successful people change their career paths multiple times during their working lives.

- **Why this myth is harmful**: This myth can cause anxiety and fear of making the wrong decisions, which can prevent you from exploring new opportunities or adapting to change. If you believe that every step of your career must be pre-planned, you will likely experience stress and a lack of joy and fulfilment in your work.
- **How to Overcome**: **Embrace flexibility** and be open to new experiences. Focus on setting short-term and long-term goals while being prepared to adjust them as you gain experience and insights. Acknowledge that your career path is not fixed and is a journey that will likely change over time.

Myth 2: "Skills Are Fixed and Cannot Be Improved."

- **The Myth:** This belief implies that your skills are static and cannot be developed or enhanced over time. This can often be related to a fixed mindset, where you believe that abilities are inherent rather than learned.
- **The Reality:** Skills can always be developed and refined. Continuous learning and development are key to career advancement and remaining relevant in a changing job market. **A growth mindset is essential**, as it views challenges as opportunities for learning and development rather than obstacles. Your skills are not fixed, and it is within your power to gain the knowledge, skills, and expertise to improve your career prospects.
- **Why this myth is harmful:** Believing this myth can limit your potential, preventing you from taking on new challenges or seeking opportunities to improve. It can also prevent you from pursuing your dreams, as you may think that some skills are beyond your reach.
- **How to Overcome**: **Regularly assess your skills** and seek opportunities for growth through courses, workshops, mentorship, and practise. Commit to a path of continuous learning to improve your abilities and remain relevant and competitive in your field.

Myth 3: "SMART Goals Are Only for Big Projects."

- **The Myth:** This misconception suggests that SMART goals (Specific, Measurable, Achievable, Relevant, and Time-bound) are only necessary for large-scale projects, not for everyday tasks or personal objectives.
- **The Reality:** SMART goals are a **valuable framework for achieving any objective**, no matter how big or small. They provide a clear roadmap and enhance focus and motivation. Using SMART goals can be a key to successfully navigate your career path.
- **Why this myth is harmful:** This myth may lead you to underestimate the value of setting clear, actionable objectives, which can cause a lack of progress towards any long-term goal. If you do not utilise the SMART framework, you may not set appropriate goals and will likely struggle to achieve them, leading to discouragement and frustration.
- **How to Overcome: Incorporate SMART goals into all aspects of career planning**, from daily tasks to long-term ambitions. Use the SMART framework to create a clear roadmap for achieving both short term and long-term career goals.

Myth 4: "Networking is Just About Collecting Contacts."

- **The Myth**: Networking is about collecting as many contacts as possible and is a superficial activity, with the purpose of "using people" for career gains.
- **The Reality**: Networking is about building **meaningful and supportive professional relationships**, which can lead to opportunities for growth, mentorship, and collaboration. The purpose of networking is to support and be supported, not a one-way street. Meaningful connections can also provide a support system during challenging times.
- **Why this myth is harmful**: Believing this myth can cause you to focus on quantity over quality and prevent you from establishing lasting relationships that can lead to genuine support and opportunities. If you believe that networking is a superficial activity, you may avoid it, causing missed opportunities.
- **How to Overcome**: Focus on building genuine connections by offering value, showing interest in others, and following up on conversations. Look for ways to collaborate, share ideas, and provide mutual support, creating genuine and helpful professional networks.

Myth 5: "Career Planning is a One-Time Event."

- **The Myth:** Career planning is something you do once and then forget about; it is a static, one-off activity rather than a continuous process.
- **The Reality:** Career planning is an **ongoing process of self-assessment, goal-setting, and adaptation**. Your goals, interests, and the job market change over time, requiring you to revisit and revise your plan. It requires continuous self-reflection and flexibility to ensure that your goals and actions are aligned with your career aspirations.
- **Why this myth is harmful**: This belief can lead to stagnation and missed opportunities, especially in a rapidly changing job market. Thinking that career planning is a one-time event can cause you to miss out on the benefits of continuous learning and professional development.
- **How to Overcome**: Schedule regular reviews of your career plan. Seek feedback and be ready to adjust your plan as needed. View career planning as a continuous journey of learning, adaptation, and growth.

Myth 6: "There is a Single 'Right' Career Path for Everyone"

- **The Myth**: That there is one perfect career path that you must pursue to achieve happiness and success, and if you deviate from this path, you will fail.
- **The Reality**: There are multiple pathways to success, and what works for one person may not work for another. **Your interests, values, and circumstances are unique, so your career path should also be unique to you**. Many people find fulfilment in unexpected careers.
- **Why this myth is harmful**: This myth can limit your options and cause you to miss the career that is truly right for you. Believing this can lead you to feel trapped in a job that does not align with your interests, skills, or values.

- **How to Overcome**: Explore different career options and don't be afraid to change paths if your current career does not fulfil you. Focus on identifying your strengths, interests, and values, and allow these to guide your path and decisions.

Myth 7: "Success is Only Defined by External Factors."

- **The Myth**: Success is solely measured by external factors, such as money, title, or social status.
- **The Reality: True success is a personal and holistic concept**, which includes inner satisfaction, balance, and the positive impact you have on others. Focus on internal motivators and consider the impact of your work on others.
- **Why this myth is harmful**: This myth can cause you to focus on superficial measures of success, rather than your own well-being and the values you hold. You may find yourself in a constant pursuit of external measures of success, which may not bring you joy or fulfilment.
- **How to Overcome**: Define success in your own terms by considering what gives you satisfaction and meaning. Strive for a balance between personal and professional life and focus on your inner fulfilment rather than seeking external validation.

By debunking these common myths about career planning, you can adopt a more flexible, realistic, and empowering approach to your professional life. Remember, your career journey is a personal one. It's a continuous process of learning, growing, and adapting to changes, both internal and external. By focusing on personal values, skill development, and strategic planning, you can navigate the complexities of the modern career landscape and achieve meaningful success.

What This Resource Guide Provides

This Career Resource Guide is designed to empower you with the tools and insights needed to navigate your professional journey confidently. It provides a comprehensive framework for effective career planning, leading you step-by-step through essential processes. You will learn to assess your skills, set actionable SMART goals, create personalised career action plans and leverage transferable skills. This guide will help you to:

- **Understand Yourself**: Reflect on your strengths, weaknesses, interests, and values to gain clarity.
- **Debunk Myths**: Overcome misconceptions about career planning that might be holding you back.
- **Assess Your Skills**: Evaluate your current skills and identify areas for development.
- **Create a Vision**: Define your career dream and develop a vision statement that guides your decisions.
- **Set SMART Goals**: Transform your aspirations into specific, measurable, achievable, relevant, and time-bound goals.
- **Build Your Network**: Develop a strong professional network to gain support and expand opportunities.

- **Develop a Comprehensive Action Plan**: Outline clear steps and tasks that lead to the achievement of your goals.
- **Embrace Continuous Learning**: Stay updated on industry trends, improve your skills, and adapt to new challenges.
- **Monitor and Adjust**: Track your progress and make necessary adjustments to your plan as needed.

Why You Need This Guide

This resource guide is not just another collection of tips; it is a comprehensive, practical, and actionable guide to help you create a career that aligns with your unique aspirations and circumstances. It provides the framework and tools you need to understand and address the issues you are facing, thereby, enabling you to accelerate and expand your career growth. Whether you are just starting out, contemplating a career shift, or wanting to take your career to the next level, this resource guide is your personal road map to achieving professional fulfilment. It emphasises the importance of self-reflection, goal setting, strategic planning, and continuous learning as the foundation for a fulfilling and successful career.

By actively engaging with this guide and committing to the steps it outlines, you can take charge of your career, overcome obstacles, and achieve your professional dreams. This is your opportunity to create a career journey that is both meaningful and rewarding.

SECTION ONE

A BOLD VISION

CHAPTER 1

Designing a Dream for Your Career

To embark on a truly fulfilling career journey, it's essential to first understand yourself at a fundamental level. This means delving into your core motivations, talents, and preferences to build a career path that resonates deeply with who you are.. By engaging in these self-exploration activities, you'll gain the clarity needed to design a professional life that brings genuine satisfaction and impact. This journey begins with a clear vision. Without a vision, you risk wandering aimlessly. This chapter will guide you through the initial, yet crucial, step of your career journey: crafting a compelling vision for your future. This vision will act as your guiding star, illuminating the path toward your aspirations. We'll explore what truly motivates you, build upon your values and passions, and give you the tools to vividly imagine your ideal professional life.

Understanding Your "Why" in Career Progression

A "dream career" is more than just achieving financial success or high prestige; it's about finding profound fulfilment, purpose, and making a meaningful impact. It is a career that aligns with your passions and values. Understanding your "why" in career progression is crucial for sustained motivation and deep satisfaction.

Your "why" is the driving force behind your career choices. It's the deep-seated motivation that fuels your actions and provides a sense of fulfilment. Understanding this "why" is essential because it ensures your career aligns with your values and passions, leading to greater satisfaction and success. It helps you to connect your daily tasks with a larger purpose and makes your professional journey meaningful. So how do you know what your why is?

- Consider these questions to uncover your "why":
    - Are you driven by a passion for your work?
    - Do you desire to make a significant impact on society?
    - Do you want to use your unique talents and skills?
    - Do you seek autonomy and control over your work?
    - Are you driven by continuous learning and growth?

Creating a Vision for Your Life: The Foundation for Career and Professional Development

Now that you're clearer on your 'why', it is time to envision what you would truly love your career to be in the future. Developing a clear vision for your career is the cornerstone of a successful and fulfilling career. This process is not a one-time event, but an ongoing journey of self-discovery. It begins with a deep dive into three fundamental pillars: your purpose, your passion, and your core values. When these elements are in harmony, your professional life becomes a powerful extension of who you are, leading to sustained motivation, resilience, and success.

Purpose: The "Why" Behind Your Work

Your purpose is the reason you exist—the unique contribution you were meant to make to the world. It's the driving force that provides a sense of direction and meaning to your career, transforming a job from a task-list into a calling. When you understand your purpose, your work becomes more than just a way to earn a living; it becomes a vehicle for positive impact.

> *"He who has a 'why' to live can bear almost any how."* — *Friedrich Nietzsche* (Nietzsche, 2008)

Nietzsch's famous quote, *"He who has a 'why' to live can bear almost any how,"* powerfully underscores the profound importance of discovering your purpose. It suggests that a life without a clear "why" is an incomplete one, and that finding your purpose is a monumental, life-defining event. It further implies that when your "why" is clear and compelling, you can withstand almost any challenge or hardship ("how"). For professionals, this means moving beyond the daily grind to find deeper meaning in their work. Having a deep understanding of their purpose can provide the mental fortitude to navigate tough deadlines, career setbacks, and difficult projects, because they are constantly anchored by the meaning behind their work.

For Example: A medical researcher named David spends years working on a cure for a rare genetic disease. The work is demanding, with long hours, failed experiments, and frequent setbacks. David's "why" is rooted in his desire to help families who have suffered from this disease. This sense of purpose keeps him going through countless failures and frustrations. His unwavering commitment eventually leads to a breakthrough that changes the course of the disease, validating Nietzsche's belief that a strong purpose can overcome almost any obstacle.

A software engineer named Alex loves building applications. After a few years, Alex feels unfulfilled. Alex realises their true purpose is to use technology to help others. Alex starts volunteering on weekends to build a platform that connects food banks with local restaurants to reduce food waste. Inspired by this work, Alex eventually leaves their job to co-found a social enterprise with the same mission, finding immense satisfaction and purpose in their new role.

Passion: The Fuel for Your Career

Passion is the energy that excites and motivates you, both inside and outside of work. It's what you would do even if you weren't getting paid for it. Aligning your career with your passion ensures that your work is not only a source of income but also a source of joy and fulfilment. When you are passionate about what you do, you are more likely to persevere through challenges, innovate, and achieve excellence.

> "*Only passions, great passions, can elevate the soul to great things.*" — Denis Diderot (Diderot, 1746)

Diderot's (Diderot, 1746) quote '"*Only passions, great passions, can elevate the soul to great things,*" elevates the concept of passion from a simple preference to a powerful, transformative force . It suggests that true excellence and groundbreaking achievements aren't born from complacency but from deep, burning passions. It aligns with the teachings of Confucius about finding purpose and fulfilment through meaningful work. Confucius believed that a person's work should be more than just a means to an end. It should be a source of personal growth and contribution to society. This perspective encourages professionals to seek roles that align with their interests, and to not just find work they like, but to pursue careers that ignite a "great passion" within them. This approach is about making their careers feel like a natural expression of their authentic selves rather than a chore, which is the only way to achieve true greatness and make a significant impact in their field.

For Example: Sarah is a project manager in a large corporation. While she is successful, she finds her work monotonous. In her free time, she is an avid gardener and loves teaching others about sustainable living. She starts a small blog and Instagram account sharing gardening tips, which quickly gains a following. She eventually enrols in a master gardener program and uses her project management skills to start a landscaping business specialising in eco-friendly designs. Her career becomes a fusion of her professional skills and her personal passion, leading to greater job satisfaction and entrepreneurial success.

Consider Lena, a talented artist, who works as a graphic designer for a marketing firm. While she's skilled, the work lacks creative freedom, and she feels her talent is being underutilised. In her spare time, she's obsessed with creating large-scale street murals, a passion she pursues with intense energy. The passion for this art form eventually leads her to leave her job. She dedicates herself fully to her murals, winning competitions and receiving commissions that allow her to create breathtaking public art. Diderot's quote rings true as her "great passion" for street art elevates her from a good graphic designer to a celebrated and impactful public artist.

Core Values: The Compass for Your Path

Passion and purpose should be mediated by core values. Your core values are the fundamental principles that guide your decisions and behaviour. They are your non-negotiable standards for how you interact with the world. Core values act as a moral compass, providing the framework for how you express your passion (what you love to do) and pursue your purpose (your reason for being). Without this mediation, passion can lead to burnout or unethical behaviour, while a sense of purpose can become disconnected from your true self and the well-being of others. Serving as a compass, your core values ensure that your career path is in alignment with your personal and professional ethics. When your work clashes with your values, it can lead to burnout, moral distress, and a sense of inauthenticity. Conversely, a career that honours your values provides a strong sense of integrity and peace of mind.

> *"Your beliefs become your thoughts, your thoughts become your words, your words become your actions, your actions become your habits, your habits become your values, your values become your destiny." — Mahatma Gandhi (Gandhi, 2019)*

Reiteration: Gandhi's powerful quote illustrates the profound ripple effect of one's values. It shows that our values are not static but are shaped by our daily choices and, in turn, shape our ultimate destiny.

This concept is echoed in other philosophies and models, such as the "See Do Get Model" introduced by Dr. Stephen Covey (Covey, 1989, 2004). Dr. Covey's "See-Do-Get" model is a framework for understanding how our perceptions influence our actions and ultimately shape our results. It highlights that our "see" (our paradigms and beliefs) dictates what we "do" (our actions), which in turn determines what we "get" (our outcomes). This cycle is continuous, with outcomes influencing future perceptions. We will discuss this model more in later sections.

For professionals, this means that every career decision, from accepting a job to the way they lead a team, should be a reflection of their deepest-held beliefs to ensure a fulfilling and ethical career path. It also means that if someone is feeling stagnant, lacking creativity or feels trapped in a job, in order to achieve different results, they may need to identify areas where their perceptions are limiting their success and consciously adjust their thoughts to align with the results they would like to have.

Realistic Example: David is offered a high-paying executive position at a company known for its aggressive business practices and a culture that prioritises profit over employee well-being. Although the salary is enticing, David's core values include integrity, transparency, and social responsibility. After careful consideration, he declines the offer, realizing that the company's values do not align with his own. Instead, he takes a lower-paying but more fulfilling role at a B Corp (Benefit Corporation) where he can lead a team that makes a positive social and environmental impact. He feels confident in his decision, knowing he stayed true to his principles.

> *Aligning your career choices with your purpose, passion, and core values leads to harmony, reduces internal conflicts, significantly increases job satisfaction, and creates a professional life that is deeply meaningful and authentic. - Dr. Stephanie Fletcher-Lartey*

Aligning your career choices with your core values leads to harmony, reduces internal conflicts, and significantly increases job satisfaction. Conversely, when a core value is violated or trespassed on, it can lead to significant suffering and make you feel miserable in your role. Core values provide context and define who a person is beyond their job title. Core values ensure that your actions are aligned with your beliefs. They provide the guardrails that keep your passion and purpose on a path that is both personally fulfilling and ethically sound. They help you make difficult decisions by providing a clear set of priorities. By intentionally exploring and integrating your purpose, passion, and core values, you can create a professional life that is not only successful by conventional standards but also deeply meaningful and authentic.

Identifying What Truly Matters to You

Your core values represent what is most important to you and form the foundation of your character and integrity. When you know them well, they act as a filtering system for what your "yeses" and "no's" are in both business and life.

So how do you identify your values? To identify your true core values, begin by selecting 3-5 words that naturally represent who you are, rather than aspirational qualities you wish to possess. Briefly define each word to understand its meaning and how you express it. Then, narrow down your list to the most essential, non-negotiable values that, if absent, would cause a noticeable shift in your being to those closest to you. Seeking feedback from close friends or family can further solidify your understanding of your core nature.

Examples of values include connection, humour, freedom, integrity, faith, joy, balance, empathy, compassion, equity, justice, teamwork, and creativity. Values can also include fairness, autonomy, helping others or service, and a commitment to continuous learning and growth.

In order to truly align your career with these principles, you must first understand your unique abilities. This journey starts with a deeper look at your strengths—the skills you possess—and, more importantly, your Zone of Genius.

In a later chapter, we will delve into a practical guide on how to conduct a thorough Self-Assessment. This will not only help you identify your strengths but also distinguish your areas of excellence from your true genius—where you can be most impactful and fulfilled.

Designing the Dream

Action Step: Crafting Your Career Dream

Envisioning your ideal career is more than just setting goals; it's a creative process of connecting with your deepest motivations. To help you get in the right frame of mind, dedicate some time to these activities. They're designed to help you listen to your inner self, get inspired, and form a vision that truly resonates.

Step 1: Set the Atmosphere

Find a quiet, private place where you won't be distracted. This is your space to dream, so make it your own. It could be a cozy chair in a quiet room, a spot in a local park, or even a library nook. The goal is to create an environment where you can relax, reflect, and get in touch with your inner voice.

Step 2: Practise Gratitude

Before you look forward, take a moment to look back and appreciate where you are. Begin with a simple practise of gratitude for your life as a whole. Then, shift your focus to your career. What professional experiences, skills, or relationships are you grateful for? Acknowledging the positive aspects of your journey so far can open your mind to new possibilities.

Step 3: Identify Your Core Values

Your core values are the fundamental principles that guide your decisions and behaviour. They are your non-negotiables. Take time to reflect on what truly matters to you. Is it integrity, freedom, creativity, or service to others? Aligning your career dream with your core values ensures that your path is one of long-term satisfaction and fulfilment.

Step 4: Explore Your Passions

What activities or subjects truly excite and energise you? Think about what you do in your free time, the books you read, or the hobbies you pursue. How can you incorporate these passions into your professional life? When you blend passion with your career, your work can become a source of genuine enjoyment and meaning.

Step 5: Visualise Your Ideal Work Environment

Close your eyes and visualise the perfect work setting. What does it look like? Do you prefer a bustling office with a collaborative team or a quiet space where you work independently? Do you thrive on a structured routine or a flexible schedule? Imagining these details helps you identify the environment where you will do your best work.

Step 6: Consider the Impact on Your Personal Life

A fulfilling career is one that supports, not consumes, your personal life. Think about how your ideal career will impact your well-being, relationships, and free time. Will it allow you to maintain a healthy work-life balance? Envisioning this harmony helps you set boundaries and make choices that lead to a truly fulfilling life.

Step 7: Document and Visualise Your Dream

Documenting your vision is a crucial step in transforming it from a fleeting thought into a tangible goal. The act of moving your dream from your mind onto paper or a screen is a powerful way to connect with it and begin the process of bringing it into reality. For some, this needs to be more than just words.

This is where a **vision board** comes in (Foy, 2015). A vision board uses images, quotes, and symbols to create a visual representation of your ideal career and life. This tangible representation serves as a daily reminder of your goals and aspirations, keeping your dream at the forefront of your mind as you take proactive steps toward achieving it.

Envisioning Your Ideal Career

It's time to envision your ideal career—your dream vocation or creative expression. Allow your imagination to soar and visualise, in vivid detail, what you would love your professional life to be. To begin, focus on your career journey. Consider these questions:

- What is the dream you have for your career?
- What would your life look like three years from now if you were living that dream?
- What are you doing?
- Who are you doing it with?
- What are you creating?
- What impact or difference are you making?

Jot down all the thoughts that come to mind, no matter how unrealistic they may seem or how different they are from your current situation. Don't worry about the "how" just yet. For now, **"set the how aside"** and liberate yourself to dream as expansively as possible. This step is crucial in unlocking the power of your mind to shape your future.

Keeping Your Vision Alive

Your career dream is not a static document; it's a living guide that requires consistent attention. To truly bring your vision into reality, it's essential to engage with it regularly—ideally on a daily basis. This consistent interaction keeps your goals top of mind and reinforces your commitment to the path you've chosen.

Here are a few powerful ways to maintain this connection:

- **Read It Aloud:** Reading your vision aloud to yourself infuses it with energy and intention. Hearing the words spoken helps to internalise the goals and reinforces your commitment to them.

- **Create an Audio or Video Recording:** Record yourself reading your vision. This allows you to listen to it while commuting, exercising, or during your morning routine. This method ensures you can connect with your dream anywhere, anytime.
- **Check In with Your Vision Board:** Make it a habit to look at your vision board every day. Let the images and quotes inspire you and remind you of the future you're working toward.
- **Carry a Wallet-Sized Version:** Create a small, wallet-sized version of your vision. Carry it with you so you can pull it out and connect with your dream no matter where you are. This simple act keeps your vision as a constant companion.

By making a habit of engaging with your vision, you're not just hoping for a better future; you're actively programming your mind to recognise opportunities and take the actions necessary to achieve your career dream.

Activity: Writing Down Your Career Dream

Now it's your turn. Take some time to write down your career dream, visualising what you want your future to look like. Start with, "I am grateful and happy that I am *"INSERT WHAT YOU DREAM OF..."* in these areas of my life. Don't censor yourself, write freely. Let your creativity flow and allow yourself to dream boldly.

"I am grateful and happy that I am *"INSERT WHAT YOU DREAM OF..."* in these areas of my life

---

Additional Activities

To further clarify your vision, complete these activities:

1. **Reflect on your values**: What is most important to you in a career? Make a list of 3-5 core values and reflect on why they are important to you. Use these values to assess whether your current career or your "dream career" aligns with them.
2. **Create a vision board**: Collect images, words, and quotes that represent your career goals and aspirations. Place it where you'll see it daily.
3. **Journal your thoughts**: Reflect on your current thoughts about your career and the potential changes you would like to make.

CHAPTER 2

Overcoming Fears and Blockers to Career

Acknowledging Discomfort with Your Current Situation

As you begin to envision your dream career, it is natural to feel a sense of longing or discomfort about your current circumstances. This discomfort can be a sign that you are ready for change and growth. **Ignoring these feelings may lead to stagnation but acknowledging them allows you to begin the process of change.** It's essential to give yourself permission to feel this discomfort and use it as motivation to move toward your goals.

In this chapter, we explore how to develop the mental fortitude needed to navigate the complexities of your professional journey and achieve your goals. The chapter focuses on acknowledging and addressing the internal barriers that may be hindering your career progress. By understanding and dismantling these blocks, you can create space for growth and empower yourself to move forward with confidence.

The Story of a Whispering Roar - Part 1

Before we dive into the principles of overcoming career barriers, I want to share a piece of my own story—a journey of longing and discontent that began in 2018.

At the time, I was an epidemiologist working in a local health district in Sydney, Australia. On paper, I had a great job. I was good at what I did, and my colleagues and I got along well. But beneath the surface, a growing sense of stagnation was setting in. I had a PhD and had been trained to the teeth in emergency preparedness, response, and management, and I felt an urgent desire to use my skills to make a bigger impact.

The initial whisper of discontent became a roar. I was no longer content to be working behind the scenes, putting out small outbreak 'fires.' I wanted something on a bigger scale where I could use my leadership skills and training.

This career dissatisfaction was further deepened by my personal life. I longed to see and spend time with my elderly mother, who lived in North America. Her health was deteriorating, and I desperately wanted her to spend time with my youngest child, who was only two years old at the time. This desire created an even greater sense of urgency.

But I was afraid of moving. My mind created 100 reasons why I couldn't apply for a job at the state level or move interstate. There was this underlying fear that people would think I was greedy to have such an amazing job and still be looking for something more. After all, everyone at work loved me! I even told myself that I didn't have the necessary experience to work at a global level and would never be able to land a job in an international organisation. My mind was full of self-doubt, despite having already sent out more than 30 applications to organisations like the WHO and other high-level regional bodies.

I worried about what my husband and children would think. I was concerned that my church family would not understand why I wanted to do this and that people would judge me as being over ambitious. I had so many thoughts about why this could not work, while at the same time the longing only intensified. The "whispering roar" was a constant reminder that I was meant for something more, but I was letting my fears and self-doubt keep me from answering that call. As we'll see, these are the very barriers that can prevent us all from stepping into our full potential. More on this story later.

Identifying Negative Mindsets and Self-Limiting Beliefs

Self-limiting beliefs, or **paradigms**, are deeply ingrained beliefs that prevent you from aligning with your career dreams and block your progress. These paradigms often manifest as negative thought patterns and can keep you stuck in your comfort zone. A helpful metaphor for this is a thermostat, which attempts to maintain a person at their existing "set point" for things like income or behaviour. To change this set point, you must adopt new thoughts and actions aligned with your vision. When these paradigms are triggered, they can activate your nervous system and produce fear, making them feel very real. However, it's crucial to remember that these are just beliefs, not truths, and they do not define who you are.

The first step to overcoming these paradigms is to recognise them.

Common Fears and Their Impact on Career Growth

People encounter various fears that can significantly hinder their career growth and acceleration. These fears are often the root cause of the self-limiting beliefs we just discussed.

- **Fear of Being Fundamentally Flawed:** This fear stems from a deep-seated belief that you are inherently inadequate. It leads to a reluctance to take on new challenges or seek promotions, as you worry about exposing your perceived flaws. This can manifest as self-sabotage and avoidance of opportunities.
- **Fear of Not Being Good Enough:** This fear can result in a constant need for external validation, making it difficult to make independent decisions or take risks. It often leads to a negative comparison of yourself to others, which limits your potential.
- **Fear of Failure:** As one of the biggest barriers to success, the fear of not meeting expectations can prevent you from taking chances, trying new things, or putting yourself forward for new opportunities.
- **Fear of Rejection:** This fear can manifest as a hesitancy to network, seek mentorship, or apply for new positions. It is a significant barrier to building a strong professional network and can hinder access to valuable opportunities.
- **Fear of Change:** This fear can create resistance to new ideas or processes within an organisation. It hinders your ability to adapt to evolving work environments and stay relevant in the job market, often leading to a preference for the status quo.
- **Fear of Success:** This fear can lead to self-sabotaging behaviours when success is within reach. It may be caused by a belief that you do not deserve success and is often coupled with a feeling of low self-worth, creating an internal conflict that prevents career progression.

How the 7 Ds Manifest in Careers

These limiting beliefs and fears often manifest as the "**7 D's**," which are common ways paradigms maintain the status quo as you move toward your vision. When the 7 D's arise, it's actually a positive sign that you are moving beyond your comfort zone, indicating that growth is occurring even as old paradigms try to pull you back to familiarity.

Here is a summarised list of the 7 D's:

- **Dissuasion:** Internal thoughts that convince you your career dream is not worth it or is simply too difficult to achieve.
- **Delay/Distraction:** Postponing important actions by focusing on less critical tasks or waiting for the "perfect" time to act.
- **DEFCON 1 (Defense Readiness Condition 1):** The body's "fight, flight, or freeze" panic response when facing fear or uncertainty about your career vision.
- **Disdain:** Dismissing new opportunities or ideas as unworthy, often rooted in feelings of blame or resentment towards others or yourself.
- **Deficiency:** Focusing on what you or your resources lack—such as money, time, or connections—to justify inaction.
- **Disqualification:** Believing you are not smart or talented enough for a new role or challenge.
- **Displacement:** Blaming external factors or other people for your lack of progress instead of taking personal responsibility.

Let's take a deeper dive into each of the 7 Ds:

1. Dissuasion

This "D" manifests as internal thoughts that convince you that your career dream is unworthy or that achieving it is simply too difficult. It's an emotional block rooted in feelings of blame and resentment, whether directed toward yourself for past mistakes or toward others for perceived slights or injustices. Releasing this focus on what bothers you is crucial for directing your energy toward what you would love to achieve.

- **Example:** A marketing manager who dreams of starting their own consulting business finds themselves thinking, "It's too saturated a market. There's no way I can compete with the established firms. I'll just stick to my stable job."

2. Delay/Distraction

This "D" combines the concepts of procrastination and avoidance. It frequently appears as seemingly practical reasons for postponing action, such as prioritizing less important tasks or waiting for a "better" or "perfect" time to act. This can create an illusion of productivity while, in reality, you are actively avoiding taking crucial steps toward your career aspirations.

- **Example:** An ambitious software developer wants to learn a new programming language to advance their career. They have all the resources but keep putting it off, telling themselves they need to first organise their email, clean their desk, or complete other less critical tasks.

3. DEFCON 1 (Defense Readiness Condition 1)

Derived from a military term for the highest alert level, this "D" is your body's "fight, flight, or freeze" panic response when you face fear or uncertainty about your career vision. Fear, in this light, is a natural response when stepping outside your known reality and is a clear indicator of making progress toward your career dreams. It signifies growth rather than a reason to stop.

- **Example:** A senior engineer is offered a project leadership role for the first time. The fear of failure is so overwhelming that they begin to experience physical symptoms like a racing heart and a feeling of dread, causing them to either turn down the opportunity (flight) or become paralyzed with anxiety (freeze).

4. Disdain

This is the voice of imposter syndrome, convincing you that you lack the necessary qualifications for your dream role. It's the belief that you are not smart enough, experienced enough, or talented enough to pursue a new challenge. It's a self-sabotaging pattern that prevents you from even attempting a new opportunity.

- **Example:** An experienced professional with a track record of success in their field feels unworthy of a leadership position. They convince themselves, "I'm not a natural leader. I'm better off as a senior analyst. Someone else is more qualified for that role."

5. Deficiency

This paradigm manifests when you operate from an underlying sense of lack or scarcity, believing that you or your resources are insufficient. This can appear as a persistent focus on perceived flaws, past mistakes, or feelings of inadequacy regarding your professional capabilities.

- **Example:** A skilled graphic designer wants to start a freelance business but is held back by the belief, "I don't have enough money to invest in a new website or marketing. I need more time to build my portfolio. I don't have the right connections."

6. Disqualification

This belief is a specific form of **imposter syndrome**, where you convince yourself that you are not capable or worthy of a new role or challenge, even if you are qualified. It's the voice of self-doubt that prevents you from even trying.

- **Example:** An experienced professional with a strong track record feels unworthy of a leadership position, thinking, "I'm not a natural leader. I'm better off as a senior analyst. Someone else is more qualified for that role."

7. Displacement

This "D" is about **externalising blame**. Instead of taking responsibility for your lack of progress, you blame external factors or other people. This prevents you from making meaningful changes because you believe the problem lies outside of you.

- **Example:** A salesperson struggling to meet their targets blames their company's outdated marketing materials, their manager for a lack of support, or the current economic climate, instead of focusing on improving their own sales techniques or prospecting efforts.

Re-patterning Your Mindset: Shifting to a Proactive State

Understanding that you can change your results by managing your thoughts is a foundational principle of leadership and personal development. This process involves shifting your mindset from one of fear to one of empowerment.

Here are some common self-limiting beliefs and how to re-pattern them using the phrase, **"Up until now..."** This phrase helps you honour your past experiences without letting them control your future.

- **Paradigm:** "I don't have enough experience to be considered for a senior role."
    - **Re-patterned:** "Up until now, I felt I lacked experience, but I am always capable of learning and growing to achieve a senior role."
- **Paradigm:** "Networking feels like using people, so I avoid it."
    - **Re-patterned:** "Up until now, networking felt transactional, but I know building relationships allows for mutual growth and opportunities."
- **Paradigm:** "If I fail at this promotion, everyone will think I'm not good enough."
    - **Re-patterned:** "Up until now, I saw failure as a setback, but I know it is a valuable learning experience that brings me closer to success."
- **Paradigm:** "I need to wait for the perfect opportunity to make a career change."
    - **Re-patterned:** "Up until now, I waited for opportunities to find me, but I now create opportunities through proactive action and positivity."
- **Paradigm:** "I must stick to my current career path to be successful because I've invested so much time here."
    - **Re-patterned:** "Up until now, I believed I needed to stick to one path, but I know diverse experiences enrich my career and open up multiple pathways to success."
- **Paradigm:** "Taking risks could jeopardise my financial security, so I must play it safe."
    - **Re-patterned:** "Up until now, I prioritised safety over growth, but I now know taking calculated risks can lead to significant growth and fulfilment."
- **Paradigm:** "My unique skills are not valued in the current market."
    - **Re-patterned:** "Up until now, I doubted my unique talents, but I know my skills and perspectives set me apart and add value."
- **Paradigm:** "Seeking help from a mentor shows I'm not capable of doing it on my own."
    - **Re-patterned:** "Up until now, I felt I had to do it alone, but I know seeking help is a strength that accelerates my personal and professional growth."
- **Paradigm:** "I need to work constantly to be seen as a top performer."
    - **Re-patterned:** "Up until now, I believed overwork was the only way to success, but I know balanced effort and self-care lead to sustainable success and happiness."
- **Paradigm:** "I'm too old to start a new business or learn a new skill."
    - **Re-patterned:** "Up until now, I felt my age was a limitation, but I know every stage of life presents unique opportunities to pursue and achieve my dreams."

The re-patterning process is critical because it gives you back your power. Instead of being paralysed by paradigms that don't serve you, you can actively choose new, empowering beliefs. This allows you to take focused action and move confidently toward your goals.

The Mind-Body Connection: Your Nervous System

The interplay between your mind and body is central to overcoming career barriers. Understanding how your nervous system works provides a powerful insight into why certain strategies, like positive thinking and visualisation, are so effective.

Your nervous system has two key states:

- **Sympathetic Nervous System (Fight-or-Flight):** This system is activated when your body perceives stress or danger, causing a physiological response that includes an increased heart rate, rapid breathing, and the release of stress hormones. This state is designed for immediate action but can contribute to a negative mindset, characterised by anxiety, fear, and a sense of being overwhelmed, if chronically activated.
- **Parasympathetic Nervous System (Rest-and-Digest):** This system works to calm the body down after a stress response. When it is dominant, it promotes a more positive and resourceful mindset, allowing for clear thinking, creativity, and a greater sense of calm and confidence.

The **"Doing Over"** paradigm, which is the tendency to react to challenges with procrastination, discouragement, distraction, or panic, is directly related to the sympathetic nervous system's activation. For example, when you feel overwhelmed by a challenging task, your sympathetic response may cause you to **Delay** or get sidetracked by **Distraction**. This constant state of sympathetic activation can hinder the creation of clear career visions and the setting of SMART goals. If you feel constantly overwhelmed, it's difficult to visualise an ideal future or take consistent steps toward achieving it.

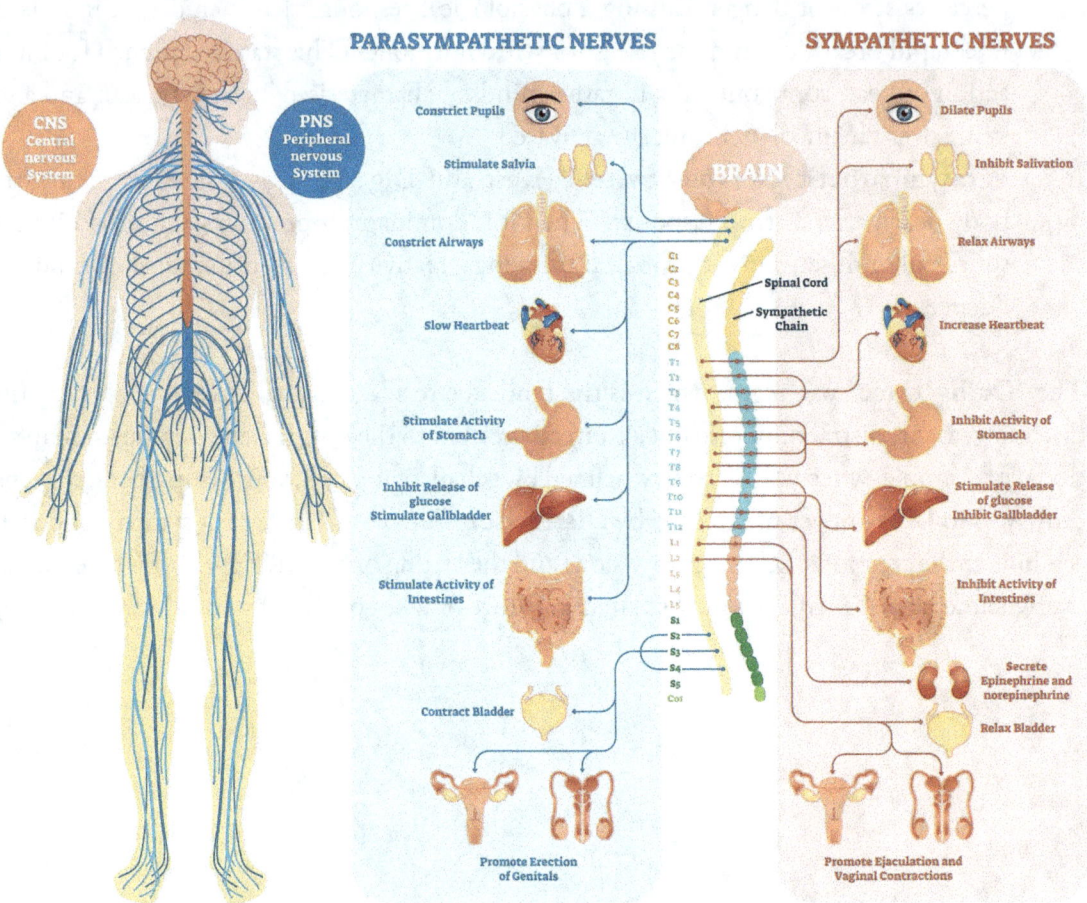

Image Licensed by Google

Practical Steps to Manage Your Nervous System

By deliberately cultivating a growth mindset and engaging in practices that activate your parasympathetic nervous system, you can reduce the power of fear and create a more positive, clear, and creative state for your career Mandino, (1968). This in turn will facilitate a more resourceful state, fostering clarity and motivation for working toward your career dreams.

Here are some practical strategies that can help you regulate your nervous system response:

- **Activate Your Parasympathetic Nervous System:** Engage this system through relaxation techniques like deep breathing and meditation. This can promote a calm and positive mindset, helping you to visualise your career goals with greater clarity and confidence.
- **Mindfulness and Visualisation:** Regular visualisation exercises can reduce stress and engage the parasympathetic nervous system, creating a mental space to work toward your career dreams. By vividly imagining your ideal future, you are training your mind and body to move toward a desired reality.
- **Practise Positive Affirmations:** Replacing negative thoughts with empowering ones helps calm the sympathetic nervous system. This promotes a growth mindset, which in turn helps you to pursue the creation of a desired career.
- **Gratitude Practises:** Starting a gratitude journal or simply noting things you're thankful for can promote relaxation and shift your focus from stress to well-being by activating the parasympathetic nervous system.
- **Consistent Action and Planning:** By breaking down large goals into smaller, manageable steps and creating detailed action plans, you reduce feelings of overwhelm. Having a plan gives you a sense of control, which reduces the activation of the sympathetic nervous system.
- **Skill Development and Networking:** By actively developing your skills and creating a strong support network, you reduce potential threats and increase your feeling of confidence. This proactive approach helps to calm the fear response and empowers you to move forward.

In summary, understanding the roles of the sympathetic and parasympathetic nervous systems provides critical insight into why strategies like positive thinking, visualisation, and planning are so important for creating and achieving your career dreams. Activating the parasympathetic nervous system through these practises helps you overcome the "Doing Over" paradigm and move toward a more empowered and fulfilling career path.

Part 2: Answering the Whispering Roar

This is the second part of my story that illustrates a resolution to the first part.

"I had mulled over this sense of longing for about a year, considering various scenarios to satisfy it. Then, one day, I got a message from a visiting preacher that resonated deeply. I fasted and prayed, and as I sought answers from my intuition, a clear message emerged: my desire to see and spend time with my elderly mother would be best served if I moved to the Caribbean or American region.

Guided by this insight, I applied for a job at the Caribbean Public Health Agency and was recruited to oversee their Communicable Disease, Health Information, and Emergencies Unit for a year. Just two weeks after starting the role, I was asked for a brief on a novel coronavirus reported from China. Within three months, a pandemic was declared.

I was strategically placed to lead the COVID-19 response for the entire organisation, supporting 26 Caribbean countries. This provided the opportunity to use all of my leadership skills and training, giving me the experiences I had longed for in my previous role in Sydney.

My willingness to step out of my comfort zone had answered the roar. It also opened further doors for me: I went on to become a Program Manager for one of Australia's leading COVID-19 research projects, which provided critical information for the government to implement pandemic public health measures. Later, I became a COVID-19 Advisor for the WHO Pacific region.

My story shows that by acknowledging and overcoming your fears, you can step out of stagnation and into a career that not only fulfils your longing but also strategically places you to make the impact you were meant to have."

Strategies to Re-pattern Your Mindset

In summary, once you are aware of your paradigms, you can begin to dismantle these beliefs and replace them with empowering ones that support your dream. Here is a summarised list of strategies to support building empowered beliefs and a growth mindset.

- **Challenge and Reframe:** When you catch a limiting thought, press "pause." Challenge its validity by asking if it's truly a fact or just a belief. Then, reframe it to align with your vision.
- **Positive Affirmations:** Use positive affirmations to reinforce self-belief. Regularly repeating affirmations, especially those you've re-patterned from your old beliefs, can help foster a growth mindset.
- **Mindfulness and Reflection:** Practise mindfulness to understand and address emotional barriers. Techniques such as meditation and journaling can help you become more aware of negative thought patterns and consciously shift your focus.
- **Visualisation Exercises:** Engage in guided visualisation to vividly imagine your ideal career. A clear mental picture of your goals can help you overcome fear and build a strong, confident mental state.
- **Embrace Failure as Learning:** Understand that setbacks are a natural part of the growth process. Embrace them as learning opportunities to build resilience and adaptability, rather than letting them reinforce old beliefs.
- **Set Realistic Milestones:** Break down your grand vision into smaller, achievable milestones. This makes the process less overwhelming and allows for steady progress, which in turn builds confidence and weakens self-doubt.
- **Celebrate Small Wins:** Acknowledge and celebrate small achievements along the way. This helps in maintaining motivation and a positive outlook, reinforcing your belief in your ability to succeed.

- **Seek Professional Guidance:** Consider working with a career coach or counsellor. They can provide personalised support and help you identify and navigate your specific challenges.
- **Network and Connect:** Build a network of like-minded individuals who can offer support, advice, and inspiration. Your community can be a powerful force for encouragement, helping you challenge negative beliefs with real-world examples of success.

Activities

Use these activities to put these strategies into practice and begin the process of mindset re-patterning.

- **Identify Your Paradigms:** Reflect on your career journey so far and list out specific paradigms or self-limiting beliefs you have faced.
- **Re-frame Your Beliefs:** Choose at least three of your self-limiting beliefs and re-frame them into empowering affirmations. Make a habit of speaking these new affirmations aloud daily.
- **Practise Mindfulness:** Spend 5 minutes in mindfulness meditation to become aware of your negative thoughts and consciously shift your focus to positive ones.
- **Journal:** Keep a journal to track your thoughts and feelings and monitor your progress in overcoming your negative patterns.
- **Identify Your Fears:** Reflect on the fears that resonate with you most (e.g., fear of failure, fear of the unknown) and list the ways they may have held you back. This awareness is the first step toward overcoming them.

By incorporating these strategies and activities, you can address both the emotional and practical aspects of your career journey, paving the way for a more fulfilling and successful path.

CHAPTER 3

Understanding Barriers

This chapter will serve as a basis to explore how individuals can overcome barriers, create a more inclusive work environment, and achieve their highest potential. Many obstacles can hinder career growth and fulfilment. These barriers can be broadly categorised as **internal** and **external**, and it's important to acknowledge and address both to unlock career potential and create a more equitable environment.

Internal Barriers

These are often rooted in our mindset and personal beliefs. These internal barriers can limit an individual's perceived potential and willingness to take risks. These psychological obstacles can significantly hinder career progression:

- **Self-Doubt:** A pervasive feeling of uncertainty regarding one's abilities and decisions. Self-doubt can undermine confidence, causing individuals to hesitate to take on new challenges or pursue their goals.
- **Imposter Syndrome:** This phenomenon occurs when high achievers feel like frauds, despite their accomplishments. They fear being exposed as incompetent or unworthy of their success.
- **Fear of Failure:** The fear of making mistakes or failing can paralyse individuals, preventing them from stepping out of their comfort zones.
- **Perfectionism:** The pursuit of perfection can be a double-edged sword. While striving for excellence is commendable, an obsession with perfection can lead to procrastination and burnout.

External Barriers

External barriers are often systemic and situational, and they can create unequal opportunities and limit career growth. These may include, but are not limited to:

- **Bias and Discrimination:** Bias based on age, gender, race, or location can create significant barriers related to unequal opportunities for career advancement. Discriminatory practises can result in unequal pay, limited access to promotions, and a lack of representation in leadership roles.

- **Lack of Resources:** Access to resources such as education, training, and professional development opportunities is crucial for career growth. A lack of these resources can hinder skill development and limit career progression.
- **Networking Opportunities:** Professional networks play a vital role in career advancement. Limited access to networking opportunities can restrict an individual's ability to connect with mentors, industry leaders, and potential employers.
- **Workplace Culture:** A toxic or unsupportive workplace culture can lead to job dissatisfaction and lack of motivation. Organisations that fail to foster an inclusive and supportive environment may struggle to retain top talent.

Common Career Obstacles and How to Overcome Them

Beyond these systemic issues, a career journey can be interrupted by situational external factors. The key is to see these as opportunities for growth.

- **Sudden Job Loss or Downsizing:** View this as a chance for a forced career reset. Take time to reflect on what you truly want next, update your skills, and rebuild your network. A job loss can be the catalyst for a more fulfilling career path.
- **Economic Downturns or Industry Disruptions:** See this as a signal to **adapt**. Use the disruption as an incentive to learn new, in-demand skills and make yourself indispensable.
- **Plateauing or Lack of Growth:** Proactively seek out new challenges. Ask for more responsibility, volunteer for special projects, or use the time to take a course. The key is to **create your own opportunities** for growth.
- **Personal Life Events and Responsibilities:** Be intentional and flexible. Use your career action plan to scale back temporarily or find a more flexible role. The lesson here is **resilience**, understanding that your career journey doesn't have to follow a linear path.

Gender and Diversity Barriers

Gender bias, racial discrimination, diversity challenges, and a lack of inclusivity can create significant hurdles in the marketplace, at work, and for career acceleration. These systemic barriers disproportionately affect women and underrepresented groups, impacting their access to opportunities, resources, and promotions.

- **Gender Bias:** Involves preconceived notions about the abilities and roles of men and women, often leading to unequal treatment.
- **Racial Discrimination:** Stems from prejudice based on race or ethnicity, leading to unequal access to jobs, pay, and promotions.
- **Diversity Challenges:** Arise from the lack of representation of diverse groups within organisations and industries.

- **Inclusivity:** A lack of inclusivity creates a hostile environment, preventing some groups from fully engaging and contributing their unique talents.

Addressing Barriers at Individual and Organisational Levels

Addressing barriers requires action at both the individual and organisational levels.

Individual Level:

- **Self-Awareness:** Individuals can benefit from self-reflection, seeking feedback, and continuous learning to overcome internal barriers and recognise their own biases.
- **Skill Development:** Cultivating critical thinking, problem-solving, and communication skills can help individuals to overcome limitations.
- **Networking:** Building a strong professional network can provide access to opportunities and support.
- **Resilience:** Developing resilience allows individuals to bounce back from setbacks and remain focused on their goals.
- **Advocacy and Inclusion:** Individuals must actively speak out against discrimination and advocate for equal opportunities.

Organisational Level:

- **Diversity and Inclusion Policies:** Organisations should implement policies that promote diversity and inclusion, including equal opportunity hiring and fair compensation.
- **Access to Resources, Training, and Education:** Ensuring access to education, training, and professional development can empower individuals to enhance their skills and advance their careers.
- **Mentorship and Sponsorship Programs:** Establishing mentorship and sponsorship programs can provide additional support and guidance for women and underrepresented groups.
- **Transparent Feedback:** Regularly providing transparent feedback based on performance can help create a culture of fairness.
- **Accountability:** Holding leadership and employees accountable for creating and maintaining a respectful and inclusive workplace.

Success Stories

There are countless examples of individuals who have shattered stereotypes and overcome barriers to achieve career success. Their stories serve as powerful reminders that with perseverance, it is possible to overcome even the most daunting obstacles. The Motivational Lounge published a series of stories (The Motivation Lounge, 2023) that serve as inspiration, demonstrating the power of perseverance, adaptability, and a clear vision in overcoming challenges and creating a more equitable and inclusive workplace.

- **Oprah Winfrey:** Oprah overcame a challenging childhood marked by poverty and abuse through determination and hard work. She started in radio and television broadcasting, eventually creating her own talk show. Oprah's success grew, leading her to launch her media company, Harpo Productions, and become a billionaire. Her resilience and dedication to helping others have made her an inspiration to millions.
- **Stephen Hawking:** Despite being diagnosed with a rare form of motor neuron disease (ALS) at 21 and given only a few years to live, Hawking defied the odds and became one of the most renowned theoretical physicists. His groundbreaking work in cosmology and black holes, along with his best-selling book "A Brief History of Time," helped popularise complex scientific concepts.
- **Malala Yousafzai:** Malala, a Pakistani activist for female education, became the youngest Nobel Prize laureate at 17. She was shot by the Taliban for advocating girls' education in her home country but survived and continued her mission. Malala has used her voice and influence to champion education and gender equality, creating the Malala Fund to provide educational opportunities to girls worldwide.
- **Nick Vujicic:** Born without limbs due to a rare disorder called tetra-amelia syndrome, Nick has never let his physical limitations hold him back. He became a motivational speaker, sharing his story and inspiring others to overcome their obstacles. Nick has written several books, founded the nonprofit organisation Life Without Limbs, and travelled the world, spreading a message of hope and perseverance.
- **Maya Angelou:** Maya Angelou faced numerous challenges, including racial discrimination, poverty, and trauma from sexual abuse. Despite these hardships, she became a celebrated poet, author, and civil rights activist. Her groundbreaking autobiography, "I Know Why the Caged Bird Sings," recounts her early life and the power of resilience in overcoming adversity.

These individuals have shown incredible resilience and determination, breaking through barriers and shattering stereotypes to achieve their dreams. Their stories serve as powerful reminders that with perseverance and courage, it is possible to overcome even the most daunting obstacles. These stories serve as inspiration, demonstrating the power of perseverance, adaptability, and a clear vision in overcoming challenges and creating a more equitable and inclusive workplace.

Conclusion

By understanding and actively addressing both internal and external barriers, you can unlock your career potential. The power to overcome these obstacles lies in a combination of self-awareness, skill development, resilience, and a commitment to creating a more equitable environment for yourself and others.

CHAPTER 4

Cultivating a Resilience Mindset

We have dived deep into paradigms, fears, and limiting beliefs as potential pitfalls for career success. Having understood these mental barriers in the previous chapter, we now want to focus on building a resilient mindset to overcome them.

Introduction

A resilient mindset is the bedrock of success. It enables you to navigate challenges, learn from setbacks, and maintain a positive outlook even when faced with adversity. Your thoughts significantly impact your actions and outcomes; therefore, developing a resilient mindset is not just beneficial but crucial for any career professional seeking growth and expansion. The power of your thoughts, combined with a **growth mindset**, can propel you toward your goals and help you overcome obstacles.

The Power of Mindset

Your mindset is the lens through which you perceive the world. It significantly influences how you approach challenges, opportunities, and your own capabilities (Trimm, 2017). As we explored in the previous chapter, your **paradigms**—the ingrained beliefs that shape your thoughts and actions—are the foundation of this mindset. A success-oriented mindset is characterised by:

- **Resilience:** The ability to bounce back from setbacks and adapt to change.
- **Positive Attitude:** Maintaining an optimistic outlook and focusing on solutions rather than problems.
- **Growth Orientation:** Believing that abilities can be developed through dedication and hard work, a concept pioneered by Carol Dweck (Dweck, 2006).

Why Mindset Matters

Mindset is more than just positive thinking; it's a fundamental driver of your actions and outcomes. Your mindset determines:

- **How you respond to challenges**: A resilient mindset sees challenges as learning opportunities, while a fixed mindset views them as insurmountable obstacles.
- **Your level of motivation**: A positive mindset fuels your drive, whereas a negative mindset can lead to discouragement and inaction.
- **Your ability to achieve goals**: A growth mindset enables you to take on new tasks and persist despite difficulties, in contrast to a fixed mindset that limits potential.

The Results Formula: From Thought to Outcome

The quality of your thoughts directly influences your feelings, actions, and results. This is a concept that was first introduced to me by Mary Morrissey, one of the foremost global life transformation teachers, in her video **'How Your Thoughts Determine Your Success'** on *The Achieve Your Goals Podcast with Hal Elrod* (Morrissey, 2022). The concept states that your thoughts lead to feelings, feelings influence actions, and actions determine your results. In order to change your outcomes, you must first change your thinking. This concept is echoed in other philosophies and models but is grounded in the "See Do Get Model" introduced by Dr. Stephen Covey (Covey, 1989, and Covey, 2004).

This "results formula" highlights how:

- **Negative thoughts** lead to negative feelings, which in turn can lead to negative actions and, ultimately, negative results. For example, if a limiting belief—or "paradigm"—like Disqualification makes you think you are not capable of a new task, you may experience anxiety. This will result in you underperforming, thus confirming your negative belief.
- **Positive thoughts** create positive feelings, which lead to positive actions and, eventually, positive results. If you approach a task with confidence and a belief in your ability to learn, you are more likely to take the necessary steps to achieve success and experience a positive outcome.

The Importance of Paying Attention to Your Thoughts

Mindfulness and self-awareness are critical to controlling your thoughts and cultivating a resilient mindset Mandino, (1968). Paying attention to your thoughts involves:

- **Recognising Negative Thought Patterns:** Identifying when you're engaging in self-doubt, criticism, or the limiting beliefs we explored earlier.
- **Challenging and Replacing Negative Thoughts:** Actively replacing negative thoughts with positive affirmations and empowering beliefs. For example, if you catch yourself thinking, "I can't do this," reframe it to, "I can learn how to do this," or "With effort and perseverance, I can learn and succeed."
- **Practising Mindfulness:** Using techniques like meditation or deep breathing to become more aware of your thoughts and feelings without judgment (Kabat-Zinn, 1994).

Growth Mindset: The Foundation for Resilience

A **growth mindset** is the belief that abilities and intelligence can be developed through dedication and hard work, contrasting with a fixed mindset, which believes these qualities are static. Adopting a growth mindset is essential for cultivating resilience because:

- It frames challenges as opportunities: Instead of being intimidated by obstacles, you view them as chances to learn and improve.
- It emphasises effort and learning: You focus on putting in the necessary work to achieve your goals and see failure as a valuable learning experience.
- It promotes perseverance: You are more likely to persist in the face of difficulties because you believe your abilities can evolve (Dweck, 2006).

Practical Examples of a Growth Mindset in a Career Professional

A career professional with a growth mindset might:

- **Seek out challenging projects:** Instead of avoiding difficult tasks, they see them as opportunities to learn new skills and demonstrate their capabilities. For example, they volunteer to lead a project in a new area, believing it will expand their knowledge and experience.
- **Embrace feedback:** They view constructive criticism as valuable information, not as an attack on their abilities, and actively seek it from peers and mentors.
- **Learn from failures:** Instead of feeling defeated by setbacks, they analyse what went wrong, adjust their approach, and try again. For example, if a marketing campaign fails, they reflect on the reasons for the failure, adjust their strategy, and use their learning to improve on the next one.
- **Continuously seek knowledge:** They engage in continuous learning activities such as online courses, seminars, and reading industry-related articles to stay relevant and competitive. They dedicate time each day or week to learning something new related to their goals.
- **View networking as a learning opportunity:** They use networking not only to make connections but also to learn from others' experiences, discover new trends and approaches, and participate in discussions.

Developing a Growth Mindset

To cultivate a growth mindset, you can:

- **Embrace challenges:** See them as chances for growth, not as a threat to your abilities.
- **Focus on learning:** Value the process of learning over the outcome of success.
- **View failures as learning opportunities:** Analyse what went wrong and use this knowledge to improve your future attempts.
- **Seek feedback:** Actively ask for feedback from peers and mentors and use it to improve.

- **Celebrate effort:** recognise and appreciate your hard work and dedication, not just your achievements.

Conclusion

Cultivating a resilient mindset is essential for navigating the complexities of career advancement and achieving your goals. By understanding the power of your thoughts, adopting a growth-oriented approach, and consistently practising mindfulness and self-awareness, you can develop the mental fortitude needed to overcome challenges, embrace change, and pursue your professional aspirations. A resilient mindset isn't just about bouncing back; it's about growing stronger and wiser with each experience. Remember, your mindset is a powerful tool – use it to shape the reality you desire.

This chapter provides an expanded and more comprehensive view of a resilient mindset, with added details on the results formula and how thoughts influence outcomes. It also gives practical examples of how a growth mindset can be applied to a career professional's life and provides ways to develop this mindset further.

Activity:

- **Reflect on a Past Failure**: Identify at least one valuable lesson you learned from a past failure, and how you might be able to use that lesson to your advantage today.
- **Practise Gratitude**: Start a gratitude journal, listing three things you're grateful for each day.
- **Identify Your Support System**: Make a list of people who encourage and support you. Reach out to them and share your career goals.

SECTION TWO

CAREER ACTION PLANNING

Section 2: Overview of Career Action Planning

Having created a vision for the career we would love and having understood the strategies to overcome fears and limiting mindsets about career growth, we can now focus on the practical steps and components for creating a robust career action plan, in keeping with that vision. Section Two will outline the detailed steps to creating a robust Career Action Plan.

This chapter introduces the concept of career planning, emphasising its importance, key components, and practical steps. Effective career planning is essential for navigating your professional journey, achieving your goals, and maximising your potential. It is a proactive and ongoing process that requires self-awareness, strategic thinking, and adaptability. By understanding and applying these principles, you can take control of your career and work toward a more fulfilling and successful professional life.

The Power of Intentional Thinking for Accelerated Career Growth:

Intentional thinking is the essential bridge that connects your vision to your actions. It's a strategy that helps individuals clarify their goals and take strategic actions to achieve them. It is built on the profound idea that your mind is separate from your physical brain, which empowers you to intentionally choose your thoughts. This intentionality accelerates goal achievement by ensuring your daily activities are aligned with your ultimate vision, so you aren't wasting time on activities that don't contribute to your success.

To fully harness the power of the mind, it is essential to replace negative thoughts with empowering ones, a practise we explored in the previous chapter. This requires the development of a growth mindset, which is crucial for viewing challenges not as insurmountable obstacles but as opportunities for learning and growth. Strategic planning, effective goal setting, and a commitment to continuous learning are all driven by this intentional approach. By consistently applying your energy to one task at a time and avoiding distractions, you can ensure that your actions are always consistent with your intentions.

This intentionality also fosters innovation and resourcefulness, as it encourages you to find creative solutions even when faced with limitations. Building and nurturing professional networks, and embracing new technologies, all become deliberate actions that expand your capacity to learn, grow, and contribute. Being intentional about leveraging your transferable skills is particularly crucial for accelerated career growth in today's ever-changing marketplace, providing a competitive advantage and a clear sense of purpose.

CHAPTER 5

Understanding Career Planning

This chapter introduces the concept of career planning, emphasising its importance, key components, and practical steps. Effective career planning is essential for navigating your professional journey, achieving your goals, and maximising your potential. It is a proactive and ongoing process that requires self-awareness, strategic thinking, and adaptability. By understanding and applying these principles, you can take control of your career and work toward a more fulfilling and successful professional life.

Why Career Planning is Essential

Career planning is a critical process that helps you set short- and long-term goals to guide your professional journey. It is not a one-time event, but an ongoing process of reflection, strategising, and action.

Definition and Importance of Career Planning

Career planning involves a structured process of self-discovery and goal setting. It's about identifying your long-term career aspirations and designing a structured, actionable path to achieve them. The process begins with a comprehensive self-assessment—evaluating your current skills, interests, and experiences—and culminates in a detailed plan to bridge the gap between where you are and where you want to be. This alignment of personal attributes with professional goals is essential for sustainable success and personal fulfilment (Holland, 1997).

A structured approach to career planning offers several key advantages. First, it enables you to be strategic about your career choices. By understanding your ultimate aspirations and strengths, you can make informed decisions about job applications, professional development, and networking that align with your long-term vision. This foresight helps you avoid roles that, while seemingly convenient, do not contribute to your ultimate goals. Second, career planning provides invaluable clarity and focus. It serves as a compass for your professional journey, helping you stay motivated and on track. Without a clear vision, it's easy to wander aimlessly and become distracted by opportunities that don't serve your purpose.

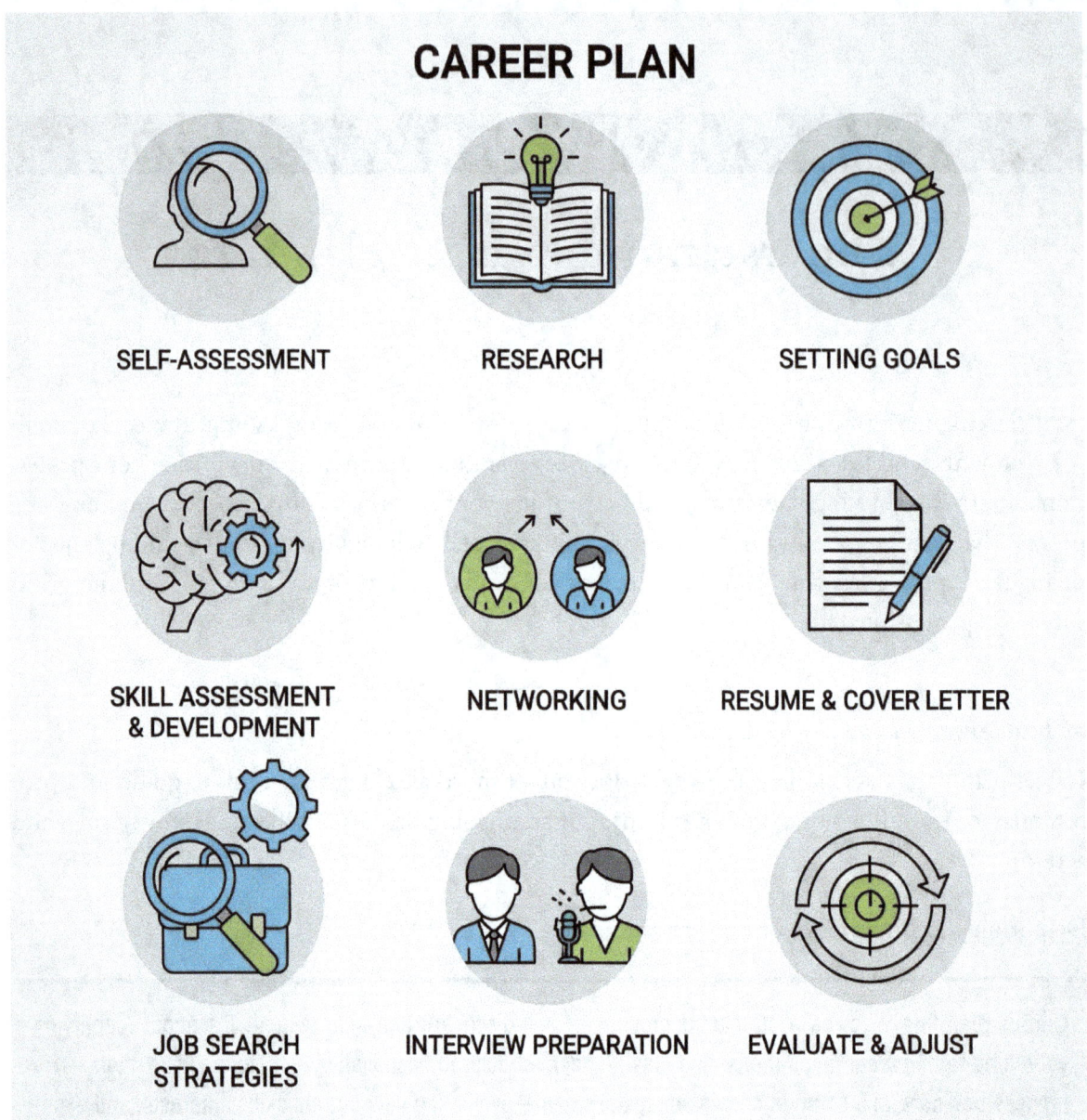

Benefits of a Well-Structured Career Action Plan

A well-structured career plan is more than just a list of goals; it is a dynamic tool that offers a multitude of benefits. It provides you with a crucial sense of **perspective**, helping you objectively assess your current position and chart a course toward where you want to be. It acts as a guide, keeping you **focused** by aligning your skills, interests, and experiences with your goals, thereby ensuring that your efforts are always purposeful.

Ultimately, a career action plan is a **road map** for success. It provides the **preparedness** and tools needed to navigate your professional journey with confidence. By breaking down your long-term aspirations into actionable, short-term steps, it transforms what may seem like an overwhelming dream into a series of achievable **milestones**. This structured approach to **goal achievement** is what enables you to turn vision into reality and build a career that is both successful and deeply satisfying.

Key Components of Career Action Planning

A comprehensive career plan includes several key components. Table 1 describes the overarching broad components of Career Action Planning.

Table 1: Components of a Career Action Plan

Overarching Component	Sub-Topics & Key Actions
Self-Assessment	Reflect on interests, strengths, and values
	Use tools like personality assessments, SWOT analysis, and skills inventories
	Practise journaling and daily reflection to review experiences and growth
Research	Explore different career paths, industries, and job roles
	Gather insights through online platforms, networks, and informational interviews
	Utilise a variety of resources: job boards, career websites, and industry publications
Setting SMART Goals	Define specific short-term and long-term career objectives
	Set **SMART** goals (Specific, Measurable, Attainable, Relevant, Time-bound)
	Focus on creating action-oriented, quantitative goals
Skill Assessment & Development	Identify skills needed for your desired career
	Enhance skills through courses, workshops, and certifications
	Embrace continuous, lifelong learning to stay current and relevant
Networking	Connect with professionals in your field of interest
	Build relationships by attending industry events and joining online groups
	Expand your network to include mentors, peers, and industry leaders

Overarching Component	Sub-Topics & Key Actions
Résumé & Cover Letter	Craft compelling documents that highlight relevant skills and achievements
	Tailor your résumé and cover letter for each specific job application
Job Search Strategies	Learn effective techniques for using job boards, company websites, and recruitment agencies
	Leverage your professional network to discover hidden job openings
Interview Preparation	Prepare for interviews by researching common questions and practising responses
	Conduct mock interviews to build confidence and refine your answers
Evaluate & Adjust	Regularly assess your progress toward your career goals
	Stay flexible and open to adapting your plan based on new insights
	Seek regular feedback from mentors and peers to refine your approach

For the purposes of demonstration, we will be following a 7-step process for the development of a career action plan as follows:

1. Self-assessment to understand your strengths, weaknesses, and interests.
2. Setting SMART career goals that are specific, measurable, achievable, realistic, and time-bound.
3. Researching career options that are suitable based on your strengths and interests.
4. Identifying skill and knowledge gaps between your current abilities and those needed to achieve your goals.
5. Developing strategies to leverage transferable skills by identifying, highlighting, and marketing them for strategic career positioning.
6. Creating a comprehensive action plan by bringing together all the previous activities.
7. Monitoring and updating your progress regularly.

Conclusion

Career planning is essential for professional success and personal satisfaction. It involves a continuous process of self-assessment, exploration, goal setting, and strategic action. By following these steps and adapting your plan as needed, you can navigate your career with clarity and purpose. Remember, your career journey is unique, and a personalised plan that aligns with your values and aspirations is key to achieving your professional dreams.

CHAPTER 6

Step 1: Skills Assessment

Unlocking Your Zone of Genius

Self-assessment is the foundational step in career planning. It's a process of deep reflection that helps you understand your unique strengths, weaknesses, interests, and potential. This clarity is essential for making informed decisions, setting realistic goals, and developing a career path that not only succeeds but also aligns with who you truly are.

By performing a thorough self-assessment, you gain an invaluable form of **self-awareness** that goes beyond simply listing skills. It helps you recognise where you naturally excel and what truly brings you energy. This process is crucial for several reasons: it helps you **identify skills and gaps** by providing a clear picture of your current capabilities; it provides **clarity for goal-setting** by aligning your professional ambitions with your personal values; and it ultimately boosts your **motivation and confidence** to pursue a path that is both meaningful and achievable. When you truly know yourself, you can make informed decisions that lead to greater satisfaction and long-term success.

A thorough self-assessment is crucial for building a successful career plan, as it aligns your professional path with your unique strengths and desires, leading to greater satisfaction and achievement. This process involves distinguishing between your "Zone of Genius" – your innate talents that feel effortless yet are highly valued by others – and your "Zone of Excellence," where you perform well but may not find genuine enjoyment. This is a core teaching I first learned from Career Coach Ashley Stahl, who emphasises the importance of operating within your Zone of Genius for fulfilment and sustainable success, a concept supported by Gallup research showing higher engagement and performance among employees utilising their strengths, while consistently working outside this zone, even in areas of excellence, can lead to burnout (Stahl, 2021).

The 10 Core Skill Sets / Zones of Genius - based on extracts from Ashley Stahl, 2021
Stephanie Fletcher-Lartey

Finding Your Zone of Genius vs. Your Zone of Excellence

A key part of your self-assessment is distinguishing between your "Zone of Excellence" and your "Zone of Genius." While you may be good at many things, your **Zone of Excellence** refers to tasks you perform well but don't genuinely enjoy. These are skills you've likely developed over time, perhaps through formal education or repeated practise. You might be praised for your competence in these areas, but they often leave you feeling drained or unfulfilled.

Your **Zone of Genius**, on the other hand, is your core skill set—the innate talents that feel effortless and energising to you, yet others find them highly valuable and even unique. This is where your passion and purpose naturally converge. Working in this zone doesn't feel like "work" in the traditional sense; it feels like an authentic expression of who you are. The career coach Ashley Stahl emphasises the profound importance of operating within this zone for sustainable success. Consistently working in your Zone of Excellence can lead to burnout, as you are operating against your natural grain. Aligning your work with your natural talents, however, can dramatically increase your job satisfaction, improve your performance, and prevent you from wasting time on a trial-and-error approach to your career (Stahl, 2021).

The 10 Core Skill Sets: A Guide to Your Genius

Based on thousands of client coaching sessions, Ashley Stahl has identified 10 core skill sets, or "Zones of Genius." These are not exhaustive, but they provide a powerful framework for beginning to identify your own innate brilliance.

- **Words:** You have a natural affinity for language. If you're an outward-focused "Words" person, you might thrive in public speaking, sales, or public relations. If you're inward-focused, you might be a natural at content creation, writing, or editing.
- **Innovation:** You're a natural ideas person—a visionary who is inspired and inventive. You are often an entrepreneur or "intrapreneur," and you thrive when you have the autonomy to make creative recommendations and build new things.
- **Builders:** You can see the big picture and possess a unique ability to create things with your hands or mind. You have strong execution energy and can bring a vision to life, from construction and mechanics to UX (user's experience) design and web development.
- **Technology:** You effortlessly work with, fix, or create technology. You have an innate ability to understand complex systems and are thrilled by the future of electronics and artificial intelligence.
- **Motion:** You're a physical mover and shaker, energised by being in physical activity or motion. This can lead to careers as a personal trainer, athlete, or a travel-related professional like a tour guide.
- **Service:** You're a natural nurturer and supporter, pulled to give and help others. Your gifts can shine as an assistant, a customer service representative, or a community manager.
- **Coordination:** You have a unique ability to think in detail and love "the little things." You excel at bringing disparate elements together to see the final product. Your genius can be found in event planning, operations management, and logistics.
- **Analysis:** You're fuelled by asking "why" and finding answers. You have a natural talent for identifying patterns and digging for information, which is perfect for researchers, intelligence professionals, and paralegals.
- **Numbers:** You possess an innate ability to work with and understand financial or quantitative data. This core skill set is key for bookkeepers, financial analysts, and investment bankers.
- **Beauty:** You have a unique skill for aesthetics and the arts. Your genius lies in creating things that are visually or audibly pleasing, a talent seen in artists, interior decorators, musicians, and makeup artists.

To begin identifying your own core skill set, reflect on past experiences and seek feedback from colleagues, supervisors, and mentors. What do they consistently praise you for? What comes easy to you, even if you don't recognise it as special?

Conducting a Self-Assessment

A self-assessment is a **vital step in understanding your capabilities and areas for improvement**. It involves a deep reflection on your past experiences, skills, and potential. This process is essential for career growth, allowing you to align your career goals with your strengths and interests, and identify areas where development is needed.

Three Key Dimensions

Beyond identifying your Zone of Genius, a complete self-assessment requires a deeper dive into three interconnected dimensions: your skills, your passions and interests, and your personality.

1. Your Skills & Strengths Inventory

Create a detailed list of your skills, categorising them for clarity.

- Technical Skills: These are the job-specific, hard skills you've acquired, such as coding languages, graphic design software, or financial modelling.
- Interpersonal Skills: Also known as soft skills, these describe how you interact with others. Examples include communication, empathy, conflict resolution, and teamwork.
- Transferable Skills: These are versatile abilities that can be applied across different jobs, industries, and life roles. Key examples include problem-solving, leadership, time management, and critical thinking.

To get started, review past performance appraisals, and ask for honest, constructive feedback from colleagues and mentors.

2. Your Passion & Interests Audit

Identify what genuinely excites and energises you. Passion is a strong inclination characterised by enthusiasm, excitement, and deep commitment. It fuels your energy, enhances creativity, and contributes significantly to your overall well-being.

- **Reflect on Your Interests:** Think about activities you find most enjoyable and fulfilling, both within and outside of work. What subjects are you naturally curious about and want to learn more?
- **Identify Your Problem-Solving "Sweet Spot":** A career can also be a vehicle for solving problems you care about. Your role in a workplace is often to provide a solution. Reflect on

the problems you have solved in your own life and the solutions you have provided for others. These can point to your unique expertise and purpose.

3. Your Personality Insights

Understanding your personality type can provide valuable insights into your ideal work environment and roles. Tools like the Myers-Briggs Type Indicator or the Holland Code can help you understand your work style and preferences.

- Introversion vs. Extroversion: For example, an individual with a "Words" core skill set may need to assess whether they are energised by public speaking and sales (an extroverted approach) or prefer content creation and writing (an introverted approach). Your energy levels and personal preferences significantly influence how you show up in your skill set.
- Work Style Preferences: Some people naturally excel at detailed tasks, while others are driven by analytical or big-picture thinking. It's also important to honour your natural physical energy levels and your body's circadian rhythm.

By integrating your Zone of Genius with a comprehensive understanding of your skills, passions, and personality, you can build a career that is not only successful but also deeply fulfilling.

Using Self-Assessment Tools

Several tools and techniques can help you gain a comprehensive understanding of your skills, strengths, and weaknesses.

- **SWOT Analysis**: A SWOT analysis is a strategic planning tool used to evaluate your **S**trengths, **W**eaknesses, **O**pportunities, and **T**hreats.
    - **Strengths**: Identify your unique assets, resources, and what you're good at.
    - **Weaknesses**: Consider areas where you need improvement.
    - **Opportunities**: List doors that are currently open to you and how your strengths can create new connections.
    - **Threats**: Identify potential hazards, competitors, and how known weaknesses can create threats.
- **Holland Code**: The Holland Code assessment helps align your interests with potential career paths.
- **Reflective Journaling**: Regularly reflect on your experiences and growth through journaling.
    - Use journaling to review your experiences and growth. Spend time reflecting on what went well and what can be improved.
    - Use tools like the Professional Core Skills Assessment Tool (developed by Dr Stephanie Fletcher-Lartey and Arete Professional Consulting and Coaching Pty Ltd.) for a comprehensive assessment and obtain a report on your possible next steps.

A template is provided in Appendix 3 that can assist you to manually conduct an assessment.

Risk Management Strategies

Risk mitigation in a career context means proactively identifying potential threats and taking steps to reduce their negative impact. Understanding and mitigating threats is essential for career stability and growth. Here are several strategies to manage risk:

- **Contingency Planning**: Develop backup plans for critical career moves. This ensures you have alternative pathways to navigate potential setbacks.
    - Develop backup plans for critical career moves.
    - For example:
        - Identify your critical career moves, and the risks associated with each move.
        - Assess the potential impact of each risk and the probability of its occurrence.
        - Prioritise risks and create contingency plans.
        - Create an action plan with timelines to reduce the likelihood and impact of the identified risks.
- **Skill Diversification**: Expand your skill sets to remain relevant when faced with industry changes. This can be achieved through workshops, online courses, or certifications.
- **Networking**: Maintain professional connections to provide support during challenging times.

Developing a Backup /Contingency Plan for Critical Career Moves

---

Career resilience is the ability to adapt, bounce back from adversity, and thrive despite challenges.

Developing a backup or contingency plan is essential to achieving career resilience, as it acts as the primary tool for **career risk mitigation**.

A backup plan provides a structured strategy to navigate unexpected setbacks and ensures continuous professional movement. It builds resilience by replacing panic with preparedness and proactive action. Specifically, it serves as your risk mitigation tool by:

- **Explicitly outlining** what you'll do if your current job ends unexpectedly or if your primary skill set becomes outdated.
- **Identifying** pre-researched lateral moves or transitions to a less demanding role/industry, mitigating the risk of burnout or a complete professional breakdown.

Steps for Developing a Robust Backup /Contingency Plan

When developing a contingency plan for your career, you must:

1. **Identify Critical Career Moves:** Clearly define the primary career moves and goals you are planning to make.
2. **Conduct a Risk Assessment:** Assess the potential risks and obstacles that could hinder these critical career moves (e.g., economic shifts, industry changes, or personal setbacks).
3. **Develop Contingency Plans:** Create alternative steps you can take if your primary plan is not successful, and outline the necessary steps and resources (e.g., emergency funds, specific training, or network connections) needed to support your contingency plan.
4. **Regularly Review and Adjust:** Be flexible and prepared to adjust your plans as circumstances, market conditions, and personal goals change over time.

Conclusion

A thorough self-assessment is the foundation of effective career planning. By using the tools and strategies discussed, you can gain valuable insights into your capabilities and develop a targeted approach to career development. Self-assessment is not a one-time event but an ongoing process of self-reflection, feedback gathering, and continuous learning. Remember to regularly revisit your self-assessment to ensure it continues to align with your career goals and aspirations. This will help you navigate your professional journey with clarity and confidence.

Activities (See Appendix 3)

- **Complete a Skills Inventory**: Using the provided table, list your specific skills, rate your proficiency (strength level), and identify areas for improvement and development. categorise your skills into technical, interpersonal, and transferable skills. This activity directly applies the self-assessment process to personal skill sets. See Appendix 3: Part 1: **Skills Inventory.**
- **Conduct a SWOT Analysis**: Use the provided links to access and complete a SWOT analysis of your current role. This involves identifying your **S**trengths, **W**eaknesses, **O**pportunities, and **T**hreats, providing a comprehensive view of your current position. Consider using both personal and career focused templates to get a comprehensive picture. See Appendix 3, Part 3: **SWOT Analysis**
- **Reflective Journaling**: Engage in reflective journaling to consider your experiences and growth. Spend time reflecting on what went well and what can be improved. Document your interests, as they will guide you towards a career path that is not only successful but also enjoyable. This practice helps in reinforcing learning and also in clarifying personal goals.
- **Review the results of the Holland Code Assessment**: Complete the Holland Code assessment and have the results handy for review in a coaching session. This will help you align your interests with potential career paths.
- **Complete the VIA Survey**: Take the VIA survey to uncover your character strengths. Review the results for further self-awareness.
- **Develop a Backup Plan**: Create a contingency plan that will serve as a backup for your critical career moves. Identify risks associated with planned career moves and create a plan with timelines to reduce the likelihood and impact of the identified risks.
- **Seek Feedback**: Actively seek feedback from colleagues and mentors and engage in open conversations. Ask specific questions to get detailed and actionable feedback. Use communication assessment tools to get objective feedback.
- **Use Self-Reflection Exercises**: Consider questions like "Which tasks do I excel at?" and "What do I enjoy doing most at work?".
- **Analyse Skills Gaps**: Following the completion of the self-assessment, analyse the skills gaps between your current abilities and the requirements of your goals.

These activities are designed to encourage a thorough self-assessment, combining practical exercises with reflective tasks. By completing these activities, individuals can gain a deeper understanding of their skills, strengths, and areas needing development.

CHAPTER 7

Steps 2-3: Career Goal Setting and Researching

Setting SMART Career Goals and Researching

The Importance of SMART Goals

Setting goals is a vital part of your career journey because it provides direction, focus, and motivation. SMART goals are essential for career action planning as they provide a clear road map for success. They ensure that your objectives are **Specific, Measurable, Achievable, Relevant, and Time-bound**, making them more effective and attainable. A well-defined career plan helps you proactively manage your career, stay prepared for opportunities, and make informed decisions, ultimately enhancing your confidence and increasing your chances of success. By using the SMART framework you can transform your professional aspirations into actionable steps.

Definition of a Goal: A goal is the intention of an activity or a plan, the state of affairs that a plan is intended to achieve. Goals are **specific, action-based, and quantitative**.

What are SMART Goals?

Definition of SMART: SMART is an acronym that stands for Specific, Measurable, Achievable, Relevant, and Time-bound.

- **Specific**: Goals should be clear and specific, defining exactly what you want to achieve. Instead of a vague goal like "I want a better job," a specific goal would be, "I want to become a marketing manager at a leading tech company".

- **Measurable**: Goals should have clear measures to track progress using numbers or other markers to assess effectiveness. For example, "I will apply to five marketing manager positions per week".
- **Achievable**: Goals should be realistic and attainable with hard work and focus. An example might be, "I will complete a marketing management certification course to improve my qualifications".
- **Relevant**: Goals should align with your broader career vision and objectives. For example, "Achieving this role will leverage my marketing skills and grow my professional network".
- **Time-bound**: Goals should have a deadline to create a sense of urgency and keep you motivated. For instance, "I will achieve this by the end of this year".

The SMART goal setting process is directly related to the career dream discussed in chapter 1, serving as a practical method for achieving that vision. While the career dream provides the overarching direction and aspiration, **SMART goals are the specific, actionable steps** that break down that dream into manageable targets. Here's how they relate:

- **Vision as a Foundation**: The career dream, as introduced in Chapter 1, acts as the foundational vision for your professional life. It is a broad, aspirational view of what you want to achieve, encompassing your purpose, passion, and values. This vision is your "guiding star," the ultimate destination you aspire to reach.
- **SMART Goals as a Road map**: SMART goals are the practical strategies and objectives you set to realise that vision. They bring clarity and structure to the process of achieving your career dreams. The SMART framework ensures that each goal is:
  - **Specific**: Clear and well-defined, focusing on what you aim to achieve.
  - **Measurable**: Quantifiable, allowing you to track your progress.
  - **Achievable**: Realistic and attainable, aligning with your resources and capabilities.
  - **Relevant**: Aligned with your overall career vision and objectives.
  - **Time-bound**: Having a clear deadline to create a sense of urgency.
- **Bridging the Gap**: The SMART goal setting process bridges the gap between your broad career dream and the concrete actions needed to make it a reality. While a vision or dream provides the "why," the SMART goal provides the "how". For example, if your career dream is to achieve financial independence, your SMART goals might include saving a specific amount of money each month or reducing debt by a certain percentage.
- **Actionable Steps**: SMART goals break down the large vision into smaller, more actionable steps. This step-by-step approach makes the overall dream seem more achievable and less overwhelming.
- **Motivation and Progress**: Achieving SMART goals can provide a sense of accomplishment and motivation. Each time a SMART goal is met, it reinforces the idea that your career dream is attainable, keeping you on course and building momentum.

- **Flexibility and Adaptability**: While the vision provides a long-term direction, the SMART goals allow for flexibility and adaptation along the way. As you progress and gain new experiences, you can adjust your SMART goals to align with your evolving vision.
- **Integration**: The career planning process emphasises that a skills gap analysis should be performed after setting SMART goals. This step ensures that all areas of your development align with the steps towards your career dream.

In summary, the relationship between the career dream and the SMART goal setting process is that the **career dream provides the destination while the SMART goals define the path**. The career dream is your big picture aspiration, and **SMART goals are the concrete milestones** that make that big picture achievable.

Structured Goal Setting

1. **Define Your Goal:** Use the SMART criteria
2. **Identify the Benefits**
3. **Recognize Potential Obstacles**
4. **Determine Necessary Skills and Knowledge**
5. **Pinpoint Supportive Individual or Groups**
6. **Develop an Action Plan**
7. **Set Milestones and Deadlines**

Structured Approach to Goal Setting

1. **Define Your Goal**: Clearly define what you aim to achieve, ensuring it aligns with your aspirations. Use the SMART criteria (Specific, Measurable, Achievable, Relevant, Time-bound). Document your SMART goal clearly.
2. **Identify the Benefits**: Reflect on the positive outcomes that achieving the goal will bring. Recognising these benefits can enhance motivation.
3. **Recognise Potential Obstacles**: Consider challenges that might hinder your progress. Identifying obstacles allows you to strategise on how to navigate them.
4. **Determine Necessary Skills and Knowledge**: Think about the skills and knowledge required to reach your goal. Understanding these prerequisites allows you to create a plan to acquire them.
5. **Pinpoint Supportive Individuals or Groups**: Identify people or groups who can support you in your journey and consider why they might be willing to help and how you can approach them for assistance.
6. **Develop an Action Plan**: Create a detailed action plan including steps to surmount challenges, leverage benefits, and gain necessary skills and knowledge.
7. **Set Milestones and Deadlines**: Establish a final deadline for your goal, along with timelines for each step of your action plan.

Examples of SMART Goals

- **Project Manager**: "Complete the PMP certification exam within six months to enhance my project management skills and increase my eligibility for promotion".

- **Marketing Specialist**: "Increase website traffic by 20% in the next three months by implementing a targeted social media strategy".

- **Commerce or Accounting Professional**: "Improve financial reporting accuracy by implementing new reconciliation procedures, reducing reporting errors by 20% in six months, by conducting training and using automated tools, which is critical for informed decisions and compliance with regulations, reviewed at the three-month mark".

- **Entrepreneur or Business professional**: "Define the target audience for my business by the end of the quarter, researching who will buy my product or service, their needs and wants, and how I can target them through my marketing efforts, which is essential for effective marketing".

- **Health Professional**

- **Goal**: "Increase patient satisfaction scores by implementing a new feedback system to collect data and make changes to improve outcomes, with a 10% increase in scores within 6 months".
- **Goal**: "Reduce patient readmission rates by developing a follow-up care program for patients with chronic conditions, with a 15% reduction within one year".
- **Goal**: "Improve clinical skills by completing an advanced certification in wound care management and applying advanced techniques in practise within six months".

- **Wellness Professional**
  - **Goal**: "Expand client base by launching a new marketing campaign, acquiring five new corporate clients within three months, growing revenue".
  - **Goal**: "Enhance client wellness outcomes, by developing a personalised 12-week fitness and nutrition program to help clients lose 5% body weight and improve fitness levels".
  - **Goal**: "Increase professional knowledge, by completing a continuing education course in stress management, and implementing at least three new stress management techniques in client sessions".

- **Teaching Professional**

  - **Goal**: "Enhance student engagement, by incorporating interactive learning tools, increasing student participation by 20% based on classroom observations and feedback within one semester".

  - **Goal**: "Improve student performance, by developing and implementing a targeted tutoring program to increase average test scores by 15% within six months".

  - **Goal**: "Develop professional skills by attending a professional development workshop on technology in the classroom and implement at least two new tech-based teaching strategies by the end of the semester".

Researching Career Options

Researching career options is a crucial step in setting up an effective career action plan. Here's a structured approach to help you dive deeper into the research process:

1. Align Goals with Skills and Interests

Research career options that align with your skills, interests, and values. Review the position descriptions, and the skills and competencies required for your desired career path. Consider your strengths, skills, and interests. Let us explore these ideas in more detail:

1. **Self-Assessment:** Start by conducting a thorough self-assessment to understand your strengths, skills, and interests. Reflect on your past experiences, both professional and personal, to identify patterns and areas where you excel.
2. **Research Career Options:** Look for career paths that align with your skills and interests. Use resources like career guides, industry reports, and professional associations to gather information about different fields.
3. **Consider Your Values** Ensure that your career choices align with your personal values and long-term goals. This alignment is crucial for long-term job satisfaction and fulfilment.
4. **Review Position Description**: Examine job descriptions for roles that interest you. Pay attention to the required skills, qualifications, and responsibilities. This will help you understand what is expected in your desired career path.
5. **Financial Considerations:** Research the salary ranges for roles you're interested in to ensure they align with your financial goals. Consider how location affects salary and job availability.
6. **Identify Skill Gaps**: Compare your current skills with those required for your desired roles. Identify any gaps and create a plan to develop those skills through training, education, or practical experience
7. **Trends and Future Outlook**: analyse market trends to stay informed about the latest trends in your field. This can help identify emerging opportunities or roles. Analysing technological changes in the industry is important. Understand how technology might be impacting your industry and what skills could be in demand in the future.

2. Use Job Boards and Career Websites

Use job boards/platforms to gather information about different career paths and opportunities.

1. **Job Boards:** Utilise job boards like:
    1. Seek https://www.seek.com.au/,
    2. Indeed https://www.indeed.com/, and
    3. LinkedIn https://www.linkedin.com/

2. **Set Up Job Alerts:** Create job alerts on these platforms to receive notifications about new job postings that match your criteria. This ensures you stay updated on relevant opportunities.
3. **Company Websites**: Visit the career sections of companies you are interested in. Many organisations post job openings directly on their websites, along with information about their work culture and values.
4. **Networking**: Connect with professionals in your desired field through LinkedIn and industry events. Networking can provide valuable insights into different career paths and help you discover opportunities that may not be advertised.
5. **Informational Interviews**: Reach out to individuals working in roles or industries you are interested in and request informational interviews. These conversations can provide firsthand insights into the day-to-day responsibilities, challenges, and rewards of different careers.
6. **Leverage artificial intelligence for job search:** All job board platforms allow you to search for jobs based on keywords, location, and industry. Most job boards like LinkedIn use artificial intelligence (AI) for enhanced job matching, automated résumé screening, and personalised candidate experiences. AI allows job seekers to use natural language searches to find roles that align with their skills and aspirations, while also enabling recruiters to screen resumes more efficiently and focus on higher-value tasks. Additionally, job seekers can use AI to create better job descriptions and analyse market trends and can assist in generating application materials like cover letters. Here are some additional benefits of harnessing AI in the Job search process for job seekers:
    1. **Smarter job search:** AI-powered tools allow you to search for jobs using natural language (e.g., "entry-level marketing jobs"), which the system then interprets to find relevant roles that might not have the exact keywords in their description.
    2. **Personalised recommendations:** AI analyses your profile, search history, and skills to provide tailored job recommendations and suggest upskilling opportunities.
    3. **Résumé and cover letter assistance:** AI tools can help you tailor your résumé to specific job descriptions by highlighting relevant skills or even generate drafts of cover letters to help you articulate your fit for the role.
    4. **Interview preparation:** You can use AI as a "coach" to practice for interviews by generating potential questions based on the STAR method or having the AI act as an adversarial interviewer.

By following these steps, you can leverage AI to effectively research and explore career options that align with your skills, interests, and values, setting a strong foundation for your career action plan.

Conclusion

In this chapter, we laid the critical groundwork for your career journey. You learned how to craft SMART goals—goals that are specific, measurable, achievable, relevant, and time-bound—and how to use them as the compass for your career. We also explored the power of research, showing you how to pinpoint career options and opportunities that truly align with your unique skills, interests, and values. The comprehensive approach outlined here—from identifying benefits and obstacles to developing action plans—is your key to creating a clear road map. As you move forward, embrace this structured approach. It's the difference between simply having a dream and actively building a future.

CHAPTER 8

Step 4: Understanding Skills Gaps

The Importance of Identifying Skills Gaps

A **skills gap analysis** is a systematic method for determining the difference between your current skill set and the skills required to achieve your career goals. This process helps you pinpoint areas where improvement or new skills are necessary, effectively bridging the gap between your current state and your desired future.

Identifying your skills gaps is crucial for strategic career development and growth. First, it helps you to **identify specific training needs**, highlighting the exact skills required to achieve your goals and allowing you to focus your development efforts efficiently. This targeted approach prevents you from wasting time on skills that won't contribute to your professional growth.

Furthermore, a skills gap analysis facilitates **personal development** by providing clear insights into your weaknesses. This self-awareness is the first step toward creating a **clear road map for acquiring the necessary skills** to advance your career. By understanding your deficiencies, you can make informed decisions about courses, certifications, and on-the-job training that will directly enhance your abilities.

Ultimately, a skills gap assessment ensures you **stay relevant in your field** and can adapt to changing job demands, helping you seize new opportunities for career advancement. It transforms a broad feeling of needing to "get better" into a specific, actionable plan.

Steps to Conduct a Skills Gap Analysis
1. List Your Current Skills

Begin by meticulously cataloguing all the skills you currently possess. Think beyond technical abilities and include your **interpersonal and transferable skills**—the soft skills you use to communicate, collaborate, and lead. Reflect on past experiences, accomplishments, and even challenges to identify abilities you might take for granted. To ensure a comprehensive list, use a **skills inventory** or a skills-based résumé template to help you categorise and catalogue your abilities. This is the foundation of your analysis, so be as thorough and honest as possible.

2. Identify Required Skills

Next, determine the specific skills needed for your career aspirations. Research is key here. Dive into job descriptions for your target roles, look at profiles of people who hold those positions on platforms like LinkedIn, and read industry insights from publications or professional associations. Look for recurring requirements and keywords to build a master list of the competencies and knowledge necessary for your desired roles. This step provides the target you'll be aiming for.

3. Compare Current Skills to Required Skills

Now, it's time to perform the core of the analysis. Objectively compare your current skill set to the list of required skills. Don't just look for a presence or absence of a skill; assess your level of proficiency. Use a rating system to quantify the gap—for example, on a scale of 1 to 5, where 1 is "no knowledge" and 5 is "expert." Pinpoint the specific areas where a discrepancy exists. This visual or documented comparison makes the skills gap tangible and easier to address.

4. Prioritise Skill Gaps

You'll likely discover multiple skill gaps. To avoid feeling overwhelmed, prioritise them. Assess the importance of each gap based on its urgency and impact.

- **High Priority:** Skills that are a non-negotiable requirement for your desired role. Without them, you cannot move forward.
- **Medium Priority:** Skills that would significantly improve your performance or make you a more competitive candidate.
- **Low Priority:** Skills that are beneficial but not essential for your immediate goals. Focusing on high-priority gaps first ensures you are dedicating your energy to the most crucial areas of development.

5. Develop a Plan to Address Skill Gaps

With a prioritised list, create a detailed action plan to bridge each gap. For each skill you need to develop, outline specific steps and a clear timeline. Your plan might include a combination of strategies:

- **Enrolling in courses or workshops:** For technical skills or specific knowledge.
- **Seeking mentorship:** To gain insight and guidance from an experienced professional.
- **Gaining practical experience:** Volunteering for projects, taking on new tasks at work, or pursuing a personal project to apply a new skill.

Be sure to identify the resources you'll need, such as books, online platforms, or training budgets. This action plan transforms the abstract idea of "upskilling" into a concrete, manageable process.

Integrating Skills Gap Assessment into Career Planning

Integrating a **skills gap assessment** into your career plan is a critical step that transforms your goals from abstract ideas into an actionable strategy. This process serves as a foundation for setting realistic and achievable career goals. By first identifying and then addressing your skill gaps, you can create a tailored development plan that is perfectly aligned with your long-term career aspirations. For professionals seeking a change in roles or careers, or aiming for a promotion, this analysis provides a clear road map. It helps outline the specific steps required to acquire new skills and bridge the gap to your desired position. This systematic approach ensures that all aspects of your development are directly connected to your career vision.

The Role of Coaching and Mentoring

Coaching and mentoring are invaluable tools for identifying and addressing skill gaps, offering personalised guidance, support, and accountability.

Coaching is a forward-focused process that helps you set specific, measurable goals and create a plan to achieve them. A coach provides regular feedback, helps you stay on track, and adjusts your development plan as needed. They empower you by asking powerful questions and helping you unlock your own potential.

Mentoring, typically provided by someone with more experience in your field, offers valuable insights and advice based on their own professional journey. A mentor can guide you through practical challenges, help you learn new skills, and share their experiences with you. They provide an external perspective, helping you see your strengths and weaknesses more clearly. They can also introduce you to new resources and networking opportunities, which is vital for career growth.

Both coaching and mentoring act as external support systems, providing an objective viewpoint that can be hard to gain on your own. They are essential for gaining clarity, staying motivated, and navigating your career path effectively.

Afrocentric Female leading a Group Coaching Session

Case Study: Administrative Assistant to Office Manager

Here is a case study demonstrating how an Administrative Assistant can conduct a skills gap analysis to pursue a promotion to Office Manager:

Background: An Administrative Assistant, let's call her Sarah, desires to be promoted to an Office Manager role within her organisation. She needs to conduct a skills gap analysis to identify areas for development and create a strategic career plan.

Step 1: List Current Skills

Sarah begins by listing her current skills, drawing on the "Skills Inventory" activities discussed in the sources. She reflects on her past experiences, accomplishments, and feedback from performance reviews.

- **Technical Skills:**
    - Proficient in Microsoft Office Suite (Word, Excel, PowerPoint).
    - Experienced with calendar management and scheduling.
    - Basic experience in filing and record-keeping.
    - Experience with inventory and placing orders.
- **Interpersonal Skills:**
    - Strong written and verbal communication.
    - Good at teamwork and collaboration.
    - Customer service and co**nflict resolution.**
    - **Active listening skills.**
- **Transferable Skills:**
    - Time management and organisation.
    - Problem-solving.
    - Attention to detail.
    - Adaptability.

Step 2: Identify Required Skills

Sarah researches the requirements for an Office Manager position by reviewing job descriptions online and speaking with current Office Managers. She notes the following key skills:

- **Technical Skills:**
    - Advanced proficiency in office management software.
    - Experience with budget management and financial tracking.
    - Knowledge of HR practises and policies.
    - Facility management and oversight.
    - Experience with roster management.
- **Interpersonal Skills:**
    - Team leadership and staff supervision.
    - Negotiation and conflict resolution skills.
    - Effective communication and presentation skills.
- **Transferable Skills:**
    - Strategic planning and decision-making.
    - Project management and coordination.
    - Delegation and task management.

Step 3: Compare Current Skills to Required Skills

Sarah compares her current skills with the requirements of the Office Manager role, identifying the following skill gaps:

- **Significant Gaps:**
    - Lack of experience in budget management.
    - Limited experience in staff supervision and leadership.
    - Lack of advanced knowledge of office management software.
- **Moderate Gaps:**
    - Basic understanding of strategic planning.
    - Limited facility management experience.
    - Basic roster management experience.

Step 4: Prioritise Skill Gaps

Sarah prioritises the identified skill gaps based on their importance for the Office Manager role and the urgency of acquiring them:

- **High Priority:**
    - Budget management – critical for overseeing office finances.
    - Staff supervision and leadership - essential for managing office staff and daily operations.
    - Advanced knowledge of office management software – needed for efficient office operations and data tracking.
- **Medium Priority:**
    - Strategic planning – necessary for setting long-term goals and operational strategies.
    - Facility management – beneficial for smooth daily operations and maintenance.
    - Roster management – essential for efficient resource allocation.

Step 5: Develop a Plan to Address Skill Gaps

Sarah develops a plan with specific, measurable, achievable, relevant, and time-bound (SMART) actions to address her skill gaps:

- **High Priority Gaps:**
    - **Budget Management:**
        - Action: Enrol in a basic accounting or budget management course (online or in-person).
        - Timeline: Complete the course within three months.
        - Measure: Completion of the course.
    - **Staff Supervision and Leadership:**

- Action: Seek opportunities to lead small team projects or volunteer to supervise interns.
- Timeline: Begin leading a project within the next two months.
- Measure: Successfully leading the team on at least one small project.
        - **Advanced Office Software:**
            - Action: Complete an online course or workshop to build expertise in office management software.
            - Timeline: Complete the course within two months.
            - Measure: Successfully completing the modules of the software training program.
- **Medium Priority Gaps:**
    - **Strategic Planning:**
        - Action: Attend workshops or webinars on strategic planning techniques.
        - Timeline: Attend one workshop per month for the next three months.
        - Measure: Completion of workshops, and application of planning in a relevant activity.
    - **Facility Management:**
        - Action: Shadow current facility managers to understand best practises or join a mentorship program.
        - Timeline: Begin shadowing a manager within the next month.
        - Measure: Completion of the shadowing program and creation of new insights based on the experience.
    - **Roster management:**
        - Action: Create a demonstration video or document showing how to perform a roster, using software that is available.
        - Timeline: Produce video/document within 1 month
        - Measure: Completion of the video/document guide

Integrating Skills Gap Assessment into Career Planning

Sarah uses her skills gap analysis as a foundation for her career plan. She will:

- Set Realistic Goals: Sarah sets a goal to apply for an Office Manager position within 12 months, aligning with the timelines set for addressing her skill gaps.
- Tailor Development: Sarah tailors her learning and development activities to focus on the skills most critical for her career advancement.
- Regular Review: Sarah commits to reviewing her plan quarterly, adjusting her goals and activities based on her progress and any new insights.

The Role of Coaching and Mentoring

Sarah seeks guidance from mentors and peers, engaging in feedback sessions to gain external perspectives. A mentor who is an experienced Office Manager can provide insights into the daily challenges and key skills needed for the role. A coach can help Sarah set clear objectives and devise a plan to achieve them and track her progress and make adjustments as needed.

Table 2: Action Plan Summary Table:

Skill Gap	Action	Timeline	Measure
Budget Management	Enrol in budget management course	3 months	Course completion
Staff Supervision and Leadership	Lead team project/volunteer to supervise interns	2 months	Successfully leading at least one small project
Advanced Office Software	Complete online course/workshop	2 months	Completion of software training program modules
Strategic Planning	Attend planning workshops/webinars	3 months	Completion of workshops, application of planning skills
Facility Management	Shadow facility manager or participate in a mentorship program.	1 month	Completion of shadowing program, insights documented
Roster management	Create video/document guide for how to complete a roster using available software	1 month	Video/document guide created

By using a strategic and well-planned approach, Sarah is equipped to address her skills gaps and work toward her goal of becoming an Office Manager. This case study demonstrates how a thorough skills gap analysis, as detailed in the provided sources, can lead to clear career progression.

In summary, understanding and bridging skill gaps is a critical component of effective career planning. By following the steps outlined in the sources and using the suggested tools, you can create a clear road map for achieving your career goals and maintaining a competitive edge in your field. Coaching and mentoring can further support this process by providing guidance and personalised feedback.

CHAPTER 9

Step 5: Leveraging Transferable Skills

Having completed our skills gap analysis, in the previous chapter, we have a clear picture of what we need to learn. But what about what we already know? In this chapter, we will go beyond identifying deficiencies and instead focus on a more advanced strategy: **leveraging transferable skills**. These are the invaluable, universally applicable abilities you have already developed. In a rapidly changing professional landscape, these skills are not just a benefit—they are your greatest tool for ensuring long-term relevance, accelerating your growth, and proactively navigating the future of work.

Understanding Transferable Skills
Definition of Transferable Skills:

Transferable skills are abilities and competencies that can be applied across different jobs, industries, and roles. These skills are not specific to any one job but are broadly useful in many work settings.

Examples of Transferable Skills: Examples of transferable skills include:

- Communication.
- Problem-solving.
- Leadership.
- Time management.
- Organisation.
- Attention to detail.
- Customer service.
- Critical thinking.
- Empathy.
- Listening skills.
- Teamwork and collaboration.
- Adaptability.

- Strategic planning and decision-making.
- Project management and coordination.
- Delegation and task management.
- Creativity and innovation.

Why Transferable Skills are Critical in the Technological Age

In today's rapidly evolving technological landscape, where automation and artificial intelligence (AI) are transforming industries, transferable skills have become even more crucial (World Economic Forum, 2023).

These skills, unlike technical skills that may become obsolete, enable individuals to adapt to new roles, technologies, and work environments. They provide a foundation for continuous learning and resilience in a dynamic job market.

- **Adaptability and Flexibility:** The ability to adapt to change is essential in a world where technology is constantly reshaping jobs.
- **Problem-solving and Critical Thinking:** As automation handles routine tasks, the demand for human problem-solving, critical analysis, and innovative thinking increases.
- **Communication and Collaboration:** Effective communication and collaboration skills are vital for teamwork, especially in global and remote work settings.
- **Human-centric skills** such as empathy and relationship building are critical for roles in customer service, management, coaching, and mentoring where human interaction is key to success.

Transferable Skills in the Age of AI

The rise of AI has led to concerns about job displacement, with many people worrying that technology will make their roles obsolete. However, a growing consensus suggests that the most successful professionals will be those who develop skills that **complement, rather than compete with, AI** (Proaction International, 2025). Rather than viewing AI as a replacement, it's more accurate to see it as an **augmentation** tool that handles data-heavy and repetitive tasks, freeing up humans to focus on more complex, creative, and strategic work (Red Hat, 2025). The skills most valuable in this new paradigm are uniquely human.

Developing these skills is vital to staying abreast of technological advancements. By focusing on areas where AI is still limited—such as emotional intelligence and ethical reasoning—you can position yourself for career longevity and success. The key is to learn to work *with* AI, using its power to enhance your own human capabilities.

Table 3: Transferable Skills in the Age of AI

Key Transferable Skill	How it Becomes More Valuable When Combined with AI
Critical Thinking	AI can process vast amounts of data, but humans must critically evaluate its output to identify biases, question assumptions, and apply ethical judgment. You become a decision-maker and a strategist, not just a data processor (SAFETY4SEA, 2025).

Creativity and Innovation	AI tools can generate thousands of ideas, but it takes human creativity to select the best concepts, refine them, and add the unique "human touch" that makes an idea truly groundbreaking. AI becomes a collaborator, not the sole creator.
Emotional Intelligence and Empathy	AI can analyse emotions, but it cannot truly feel or understand human context. This skill is critical for leadership, negotiation, customer service, and building trust in a world that is becoming increasingly automated (Edwards, 2025).
Strategic Planning	AI can forecast trends and analyse data, but humans must use that information to develop long-term vision and purpose. You move from number-crunching to big-picture thinking, crafting a vision that AI cannot create on its own.
Complex Problem-Solving	AI can find patterns in data, but it cannot solve ambiguous, ill-defined problems that require abstract thinking and collaboration. Your ability to troubleshoot and address unique challenges becomes more valuable than ever.
Communication and Collaboration	As AI becomes integrated into workflows, effective communication is essential for explaining AI outputs to non-technical colleagues and collaborating with teams to implement AI-driven solutions (Proaction International, 2025).

Combining transferable skills with intentional thinking

Leveraging transferable skills and intentional thinking are both strategic approaches that can significantly contribute to career growth and acceleration. Combining transferable skills with intentional thinking leads to accelerated career growth. Intentionality provides the focus and clarity needed to leverage transferable skills effectively, by identifying the best ways to apply them in career advancement and new opportunities. Additionally, intentional thinking helps you cultivate a mindset conducive to continuous learning and innovation, which is essential for long-term career success. In the technological age, where change is constant, the combination of transferable skills and intentional thinking empowers individuals to navigate complexity, adapt to change, and drive their own career trajectory. By proactively identifying and marketing your transferable skills, aligning your actions with your vision, and continuously pursuing growth opportunities, you can accelerate your career and achieve your professional aspirations.

Leveraging Transferable Skills

To obtain a competitive advantage for accelerated career growth involves leveraging transferable skills by identifying, highlighting and marketing them. Identifying transferable skills involves reflecting on past experiences, looking for common themes, and using checklists. Highlighting these skills requires providing examples, relating them to job requirements, and keeping a skills notebook. Marketing transferable skills strategically involves tailoring your résumé, cover letter, and LinkedIn profile to emphasise relevant skills and using your network to identify job opportunities. Building a portfolio or personal website can also showcase these skills in action. Let us examine these steps in more detail.

Identify Transferable Skills

- **Reflect on Past Experiences:** Think about previous jobs, volunteer work, projects, and hobbies. Consider family-related tasks as well, as they could contribute to filling gaps at work. Identify the skills used in these activities that contributed to your success.
- **Look for Common Themes:** Identify common skills you have used in different contexts. For example, if you have been involved in team projects in various settings, teamwork and collaboration are likely transferable skills. If you've prepared presentations, managed social media, or recorded videos, these indicate communication skills, content creation, and creative skill sets.
- **Use Checklists to Identify Skills:** Utilise tools like the JSWA-personal-transferable-skills checklist, the SEEK Transferable Skills Checklist or a skills assessment template to help identify your skills. categorise these skills into technical, interpersonal, and transferable skills.

Highlighting Transferable Skills

- **Use Examples to Discuss Skills:** Be prepared to discuss your transferable skills with specific examples of how you have used them in previous roles. A great way to share your experience is by using the **STAR method**.
- The **STAR method** (Situation, Task, Action, Result) is a structured approach to answering behavioural interview questions by providing specific examples of past experiences. Here's how you can use the STAR method to showcase your skills in an interview:
- **Situation:** Describe the context within which you performed a task or faced a challenge at work. Be specific about the situation to give the interviewer a clear understanding of the context.
    - Example: "In my previous role as a project manager at XYZ Company, we were tasked with launching a new product within a tight deadline."
- **Task:** Explain the actual task or responsibility you had in that situation. This helps the interviewer understand your role and what was expected of you.

- Example: "My responsibility was to coordinate the efforts of the marketing, design, and development teams to ensure the product launch was successful and on time."
- **Action:** Describe the specific actions you took to address the task or challenge. Focus on what you did, how you did it, and why you chose those actions.
    - Example: "I organised regular cross-functional team meetings to ensure everyone was aligned and on track. I also implemented a project management tool to monitor progress and address any issues promptly."
- **Result:** Share the outcomes or results of your actions. Quantify the results if possible to demonstrate the impact of your efforts.
    - Example: "As a result of my efforts, we successfully launched the product on time, which led to a 20% increase in sales within the first quarter. The project was also praised by senior management for its smooth execution."
- **Putting It All Together:** When asked a question like, "Can you give an example of a time when you successfully managed a project?" you can respond using the STAR method:
- Example: "In my previous role as a project manager at XYZ Company, we were tasked with launching a new product within a tight deadline. My responsibility was to coordinate the efforts of the marketing, design, and development teams to ensure the product launch was successful and on time. I organised regular cross-functional team meetings to ensure everyone was aligned and on track. I also implemented a project management tool to monitor progress and address any issues promptly. As a result of my efforts, we successfully launched the product on time, which led to a 20% increase in sales within the first quarter. The project was also praised by senior management for its smooth execution."
- By using the STAR method, you can provide clear, concise, and compelling examples of how you have successfully applied your skills in various situations.
- **Relate Skills to the Job:** When applying for a new position, relate your transferable skills to the requirements of the job to demonstrate how these skills will help you succeed in the new role.
- **Use a Skills Notebook:** Keep a notebook with various examples of how you have used these skills in previous roles. This can be a helpful reference when you go for interviews.

Marketing Transferable Skills

- **Tailor Messaging and Networking:**
    - Customise your résumé, cover letter, and LinkedIn profile to emphasise the transferable skills most relevant to the job you are targeting.
    - Use your network to understand what skills are valued in your desired roles and industries.
    - Attend industry events, join professional groups, and connect with people who can provide insights and opportunities related to your transferable skills.
- **Use LinkedIn for Visibility:**
    - Create and update your LinkedIn profile, highlighting your top skills.
    - Use LinkedIn to connect with industry professionals.

- Share posts and engage with content relevant to your area of expertise.
- **Showcase Skills in Action:** Build a portfolio or personal website to showcase examples of your work that highlight your transferable skills.

Case Study No 1: Leveraging Transferable Skills - Customer Service Representative
Scenario:

A Customer Service Representative, named Alex, has been working in a call centre environment for several years. While they are proficient in their role, they want to transition to a different career path, such as project coordination or a role in a different industry, or a move into a more strategic role within the same industry. Alex wants to understand and leverage their transferable skills to achieve this goal.

Step 1: Identifying Transferable Skills

Alex begins by reflecting on their past experiences. They consider the tasks they perform daily and identify their key strengths. Using the skills inventory approach, Alex categorises their skills. For example, they use a skills assessment table or a checklist to ensure they have considered the full range of skills they may have. They identify the following as their most relevant transferable skills:

- **Communication:** Alex regularly interacts with customers, which involves active listening, explaining complex information, and writing clear emails and chat responses.
- **Problem-solving:** Alex handles customer issues and complaints and finds effective solutions.
- **Time management:** They manage multiple customer interactions daily, needing to prioritise and remain organised.
- **Empathy:** They understand and respond to customer concerns with compassion and understanding.
- **Adaptability:** Alex is able to quickly adapt to changing customer needs and situations.
- **Attention to Detail:** Accurately records customer information and details of their requests.

To get a broader understanding of their skills, Alex asks for feedback from colleagues, supervisors, and mentors. They may get some additional insights into their strengths and also areas they may not have considered.

Step 2: Highlighting Transferable Skills

After identifying their key transferable skills, Alex focuses on highlighting them effectively on their résumé and cover letter.

- **Résumé:** Alex includes a summary at the top of their résumé, emphasizing skills such as "Skilled in communication, problem-solving, and time management. Proven experience in managing customer relationships and resolving issues efficiently". Under each job role, they emphasise how they applied their skills, providing specific examples of their impact and contribution.

- **Cover Letter:** Alex tailors their cover letter to showcase how their communication skills, problem-solving abilities, and customer service experience make them a strong candidate for roles in other fields. They focus on how these skills are relevant to the job, as discussed in the sources. Alex also shows how their skills will benefit the potential employer.
- **Interviews:** Alex prepares by writing down examples of situations where they have used their transferable skills, highlighting any positive outcomes, as suggested in the sources.

Step 3: Marketing Transferable Skills for Strategic Career Positioning

Alex creates a LinkedIn profile and a personal brand statement, marketing these skills strategically for career positioning.

- **LinkedIn Profile:** Alex's LinkedIn profile highlights their top 10 skills, including communication, problem-solving, and time management. Alex creates a professional statement about how their skills set them apart in the customer service industry, and how they can be utilised in any industry or job role.
- **Networking:** Alex begins to strategically network with professionals in fields that interest them. They attend industry events and join relevant groups on LinkedIn to build connections and to understand what other skills might be valued in those roles.
- **Personal Website:** Alex creates a personal website or online portfolio with examples of their work, highlighting their ability to communicate effectively through written material.
- **Tailoring Messaging:** Alex tailors their résumé, cover letter, and LinkedIn profile to emphasise the transferable skills most relevant to their target job roles, using specific keywords. For instance, when applying for a project coordinator role, they highlight their ability to manage multiple tasks and communicate clearly.

Example Application

- To demonstrate these steps in practise, Alex takes the following approach when applying for a Project Coordinator role:
    - In the skills section of their résumé, they explicitly state "Proficient in communication, problem-solving, and time management."
    - In the "Experience" section, they elaborate:
        - **Communication:** "Communicated with diverse customer base to understand needs and provide effective solutions."
        - **Problem-Solving:** "Resolved a wide variety of customer issues, demonstrating critical thinking and effective solutions."
        - **Time Management:** "Managed multiple customer inquiries, prioritising tasks effectively and ensuring timely resolutions."
    - In their cover letter, they state: "My experience in managing complex customer interactions has provided me with strong time management and communication skills, which I believe would be a valuable asset to a project coordination role."

- They use the **STAR method** in interviews to illustrate these skills, stating the situation, task, action and result of past experiences.

Outcomes

- By effectively identifying, highlighting, and marketing their transferable skills, Alex is able to successfully position themselves for a project coordinator role, demonstrating how these skills are directly applicable to other industries and different job roles.
- Alex is now working in a role that they are passionate about and are more confident about their career path.

This case study demonstrates how a Customer Service Representative can leverage their transferable skills for career advancement by following the steps outlined in the sources, and our conversation history: **identifying** the skills gained in their current role, **highlighting** these skills in their application materials, and **marketing** these skills for a strategic career transition. This approach not only helps in securing a new role but also builds confidence and opens doors to new opportunities.

Case Study No 2: Leveraging Environmental Health Skills for a Research, Monitoring, and Evaluation Officer role at a Public Health NGO

Scenario:

Stephanie has a background as an Environmental Health Officer, where she developed skills in surveying, data analysis, critical analysis, case investigations, monitoring and evaluation, report writing, and research. In her role, she also worked closely with community-based organisations to develop plans to solve health problems at the community level and strategically set up community-based health committees to lead community-based projects. She is now seeking a role as a Research, Monitoring, and Evaluation Officer in a public health NGO that works closely with community groups to provide health solutions and wants to understand how her existing skills are **transferable** and how she can highlight and market them.

Step 1: Identifying Transferable Skills

- Stephanie starts by reflecting on her past experiences, considering her day-to-day tasks, and uses a skills inventory to categorise her skills, identifying the following as most relevant:
    - **Data Analysis**: Stephanie has experience in collecting and analysing data from surveys and case investigations, directly applicable to research and M&E roles.
    - **Critical Analysis and Appraisal**: Stephanie has experience in evaluating data and situations, which is crucial for assessing program effectiveness.
    - **Surveying**: She has experience in designing and conducting surveys and gathering relevant data.
    - **Case Investigations**: Stephanie has experience investigating health cases, including data gathering, analysis, and reporting outcomes.
    - **Monitoring and Evaluation**: Stephanie has experience tracking programs and evaluating their impact.
    - **Report Writing**: Stephanie regularly documents her findings in reports.
    - **Research**: Stephanie is familiar with research methodologies.
    - **Community Engagement:** Stephanie has experience working closely with community-based organisations, co-developing health plans, and establishing community-based health committees. This demonstrates her ability to work collaboratively with communities to co-design and implement solutions.
    - **Project Management**: Stephanie has experience in setting up community based health committees to lead projects, showing her ability to plan, organise, and manage projects at the community level.
    - **Stakeholder Management**: Stephanie has experience in engaging different stakeholders including community groups and government agencies.

- ◦ **Capacity Building**: Stephanie has experience in building community leadership capacity by establishing community-based health committees and empowering them to manage community-based projects.
- Stephanie recognises the importance of gaining **constructive feedback** and speaks to her mentors and former colleagues to further validate her skills.

Step 2: Highlighting Transferable Skills

- Stephanie focuses on effectively highlighting these **transferable skills** on her résumé, cover letter, and in interviews.
    - ◦ **Résumé**: Stephanie includes a summary that emphasises her skills in community engagement, data analysis, and monitoring and evaluation and her understanding of environmental health and its links to public health. In the experience section, she emphasises how she has used her skills in her previous roles providing specific examples.
    - ◦ **Cover Letter**: Stephanie uses the cover letter to demonstrate how her skills in data analysis, research and monitoring and evaluation as well as her experience working directly with community-based organisations and community health committees are directly applicable to a Research, Monitoring, and Evaluation Officer position in a public health NGO. She shows how her experience aligns with the requirements of the new role.
    - ◦ **Interviews**: Stephanie prepares to provide examples of situations where she has successfully applied her skills, using the **STAR method**. She demonstrates her **adaptability**, **problem-solving**, community engagement, and project management skills.

Step 3: Marketing Transferable Skills for Strategic Career Positioning

- Stephanie uses the principles of strategic career positioning by highlighting her skills in her new role, on her online profiles and during networking opportunities:
    - ◦ **LinkedIn Profile**: Stephanie optimises her LinkedIn profile, clearly stating her experience with a focus on community engagement, data analysis, M&E, and her experience in environmental health. She uses keywords relevant to the M&E field and highlights her experience in working directly with communities.
    - ◦ **Networking:** She leverages existing networks, attends relevant industry events and webinars, and joins LinkedIn groups to connect with professionals in the public health M&E field. She seeks to connect with professionals working directly with community groups to better understand how community engagement can be measured.
    - ◦ **Portfolio**: She creates a portfolio of her previous work including research reports, surveys, and examples of community health plans that she has co-developed with communities and reports on projects led by the community based health committees.
    - ◦ **Personal Branding**: Stephanie develops a personal brand statement that highlights her skills in research, community engagement and her unique experience blending en-

vironmental health and community engagement to differentiate herself from other candidates.

Example Application

- When applying for a Research, Monitoring, and Evaluation Officer position at a public health NGO, Stephanie uses the following:
    - **Résumé Summary**: Includes the statement "Experienced Environmental Health Officer skilled in data analysis, research, monitoring and evaluation, community engagement and project management; passionate about working with community groups to improve public health."
    - **Experience Section**:
        - **Community Engagement**: "Collaborated with community-based organisations to co-develop and implement community health plans." She also highlights her "Experience in setting up community-based health committees and empowering them to lead local health projects," and "Experience in engaging with different stakeholders including community groups and government agencies."
        - **Project Management:** "Led the establishment of community health committees, providing support and guidance to ensure successful project outcomes."
        - **Data Analysis:** "Conducted statistical analysis on environmental health data, leading to actionable recommendations for public health interventions."
        - **Surveying**: Designed and conducted surveys to assess environmental health risks in communities.
        - **Case Investigations:** "Investigated complex health cases, gathering and analysing data to identify key trends and develop intervention strategies".
        - **Monitoring and Evaluation:** "Monitored the implementation of environmental health programs and evaluated their effectiveness to ensure that they were achieving program goals and objectives."
        - **Research**: She states that she has "Experience in conducting research for environmental health initiatives, including the creation of reports based on her findings"
    - **Cover Letter**: She emphasises that, "My background in environmental health and my experience in working closely with community-based organisations has provided me with a strong foundation in research, monitoring and evaluation as well as deep understanding of the critical role that communities play in public health. I am eager to apply these skills to contribute to your organisation's mission of empowering communities to improve health outcomes."
    - **Interviews**: She shares specific examples where her data analysis skills helped improve the effectiveness of an environmental health intervention, and how she successfully set up a community-based health committee which led to community led projects. She demonstrates her ability to achieve results, her community engagement skills, and her project management experience.

Outcomes

1. By effectively identifying, highlighting, and marketing her transferable skills in data analysis, research, monitoring and evaluation, project management and community engagement, Stephanie successfully positions herself for the Research, Monitoring, and Evaluation Officer role. She is able to articulate how her skills and experience as an Environmental Health Officer are directly applicable and valuable to her new role in public health and also how her skills in community engagement and project management makes her a uniquely strong candidate.
2. Stephanie is able to bring a unique perspective to the NGO, especially as it is working directly with community groups as she has a solid understanding of working collaboratively with community-based organisations.

This case study shows how Stephanie, with her experience as an Environmental Health Officer and her community engagement work, can make a successful career transition to a Research, Monitoring, and Evaluation Officer role in a public health NGO. By **self-reflecting,** using tools for skill assessments, engaging in strategic networking, showcasing her experience, and marketing her unique blend of skills, Stephanie is well-positioned to excel in her new role. She can leverage her skills in data analysis, research and monitoring and evaluation, as well as her experience in community engagement and project management. She can also demonstrate her value to the potential employer as someone who can build effective relationships with community groups and also has a solid understanding of research, M&E, data analysis and report writing.

Conclusion: Embracing a Strategic Advantage

In today's dynamic world, transferable skills are your most powerful asset. They are the universal currency of the modern workforce, allowing you to adapt, pivot, and thrive in any role or industry. By intentionally combining these skills with a growth mindset and a proactive approach to technology, you transform yourself from a passive participant into a strategic driver of your own career.

Embracing transferable skills, coupled with intentional thinking and a willingness to work alongside AI, gives you a clear and superior advantage. It's about recognising that as technology takes on the technical and routine tasks, your uniquely human skills—creativity, critical thinking, empathy, and strategic communication—become more valuable than ever.

This chapter has provided you with the tools to identify, highlight, and market these skills. As you move forward, remember to continuously monitor the technological landscape, staying curious about future developments and how they can augment your abilities. By strategically applying your transferable skills, you can not only secure your place in the future of work but also build a career that is both resilient and deeply fulfilling.

CHAPTER 10

Step 6: Creating a Comprehensive Career Plan

Understanding the Components of an Action Plan

A career action plan is more than just a list of goals; it is a detailed road map that transforms your aspirations into actionable steps. It is a strategic and structured approach to your professional journey, moving beyond a passive hope for success to an intentional plan for career development and advancement. By outlining each phase, you are not simply reacting to opportunities but proactively creating a path toward the career you envision.

This chapter will guide you through the process of building your own comprehensive plan, providing the framework to turn your vision into a tangible reality.

From Analysis to Action: Your Step-by-Step Guide

In our work together, we have successfully completed the first five steps of the career action plan process, gathering all the necessary data to build your blueprint for success.

- **Step 1: Self-Assessment** - We uncovered your core strengths, weaknesses, and interests.
- **Step 2: SMART Goals** - We defined a clear vision for your career with specific, measurable goals.
- **Step 3: Career Research** - We identified a path that aligns with your passions and skills.
- **Step 4: Skills Gap Analysis** - We pinpointed the skills you need to acquire.
- **Step 5: Transferable Skills** - We strategised on how to leverage the skills you already possess.

Steps in Creating A Career Action Plan
Stephanie Fletcher-Lartey

Now, we have arrived at the critical point of **Step 6: Creating the Comprehensive Action Plan**. This is where we bring together all the insights and findings from the previous steps to build your official road map. This final plan will be a cohesive, living document that transforms your self-discovery and research into actionable tasks, guiding you directly toward your career goals.

Understanding the Components of an Action Plan

An effective career plan is built on a few core components that ensure clarity, accountability, and progress. Your plan should include:

- A **well-defined description** of the goal you want to achieve.

- The **specific tasks or steps** needed to reach that goal.
- An assigned **person responsible** for each task (in your case, that's you!).
- Clear **deadlines and milestones** for task completion.
- A list of **resources** needed to complete the tasks.
- A method to **track and evaluate** your progress.

The key to a successful action plan is translating your broad goals and research into concrete, manageable tasks.

1. Translate Your SMART Goals into Actionable Steps

Break down your long-term vision into short-term, actionable steps. For example, if your SMART goal is to "Obtain a project management certification by December 2025," your plan would include a series of smaller, sequential steps:

- Goal: Obtain a project management certification by December 2025.
- Action Steps:
    - Research and select an online PM course.
    - Enrol in the course and set a completion deadline.
    - Schedule time each week to study.
    - Set a date to take the certification exam.
- Timeline: "Complete the PM course by September 2025."
- Resources: "Access to an online course platform, study materials."
- Tracking: "Monthly review sessions."

Remember to celebrate small achievements along the way to build momentum and confidence.

2. Utilise Tools and Resources

To keep your plan organised and on track, consider using a variety of tools.

- Spreadsheets: For a basic but highly effective plan, a spreadsheet program like MS Excel or Google Sheets is perfect. You can create columns for your goals, specific tasks, deadlines, and a "completion" column to check off your progress. You can even add a column for necessary resources or follow-up notes.
- Project Management Apps: For more complex plans, apps like Trello or Asana can help you organise tasks, set deadlines, and manage your projects visually.
- Professional Platforms: Platforms like LinkedIn can be used to identify new skills to build, find courses, and network with professionals who can help guide you.

By following these steps, you can ensure your career action plan is a dynamic, living tool that provides clarity and purpose, helping you achieve your professional aspirations.

Organising Your Comprehensive Career Action Plan Document

Your document should be organised into distinct sections that reflect the work you've already completed.

Section 1: Background and Foundation

This section serves as your reference point, summarising all the data you gathered in the initial steps.

- **Self-Assessment Summary:** Start with a brief summary of your core strengths, weaknesses, skills, interests, and values from your self-assessment (Step 1). This reminds you of your starting point and what truly motivates you.
- **Career Goals:** Clearly state your **SMART** goals, including your long-term vision and any short-term objectives you established (Step 2).
- **Career Path Research:** Include a summary of your research findings (Step 3). This could be a list of potential job titles, industries, or companies you've identified, along with key insights about those roles.
- **Skills Analysis:** This is where you document the results of your skills gap analysis (Step 4). List the key skills you need to develop and how you plan to leverage your existing transferable skills (Step 5), especially in the age of AI.

Section 2: The Action Plan (*Tabular Format*)

This is the core of your document, where you translate your research and findings into a practical plan. A table is an ideal format for this, as it allows for clear organisation and easy tracking (See additional template in Appendix 7).

Here is a Suggested Template that can be used.

Example Action Plan (Tabular Format)

Career Goal	Action Step	Start Date	Deadline	Resources Needed	Status	Notes
Obtain Project Management Certification by 2026	Research and choose a certification course (PMP, CAPM, etc.)	[Date]	[Date]	Internet access, course reviews	Not Started	Look for courses with flexible schedules.
	Enrol in the course			Course fee, computer		
	Complete the coursework and pass the exam			Study time, study materials		
Transition to a Data Analyst Role	Take an online course on Python for data analysis			Coursera subscription		Find a course with hands-on projects.
	Complete a personal project to showcase skills			Data sets, GitHub account		Choose a project relevant to my target industry.

Section 3: Monitoring and Review

A career action plan isn't a one-and-done task; it's a **living document**. This final section is dedicated to your ongoing commitment to monitoring and adapting your progress. Think of it as the feedback loop that ensures your plan stays on track and remains relevant as you and the world around you change.

Your plan should incorporate the following elements:

- **Review Schedule**: Set a consistent schedule for reviewing your progress—whether it's monthly, quarterly, or annually. These check-ins are crucial for staying accountable.
- **Progress Log**: Create a dedicated space to record your achievements, note any challenges you've faced, and jot down lessons learned. This log will serve as a valuable record of your journey and provide key insights for future decisions.
- **Plan Updates**: Remember, your plan is flexible. Be prepared to update goals, timelines, or action steps based on new information, skills acquired or shifts in your career aspirations.

This monitoring process is the crucial link between planning and achievement. In the next chapter, we'll dive into the detailed steps for keeping your plan dynamic and effective. We will cover:

1. Setting Milestones and Review Timelines
2. Tracking Your Progress
3. Evaluating Current Strategies
4. Identifying Obstacles and Challenges
5. Adapting and Modifying Goals
6. Developing New Skills
7. Reinforcing Motivation

Example: Career Action Plan for Administrative Assistant to Office Manager

This example utilises the action plan template, demonstrating how an administrative assistant can transition into an office manager role. It includes specific steps, timelines, resources, and tracking methods. The plan incorporates **SMART goals** and addresses the **skills gap analysis** results from earlier.

Table 4: Career Action Plan for Administrative Assistant to Office Manager

Career Goal	Action Step	Start Date	Deadline	Resources Needed
Skill Gap: Learn Staff Supervision	Enrol in staff super-vision training program	Jul-24	Aug 31, 2024	Online training platform, training fees
	Complete the training program modules	Sep 1, 2024	Sep 30, 2024	Training materials, access to online course
	Seek opportunities to supervise junior staff	Oct 1, 2024	Ongoing	Internal team, senior manager support
Skill Gap: Advanced Office Management Software	Research advanced office management software courses	Jul 1, 2024	Jul 15, 2024	Online search tools, review platforms
	Enrol in a selected course	Jul 16, 2024	Aug 15, 2024	Online enrolment platform, fees
	Complete the course	Aug 16, 2024	Sep 30, 2024	Access to course modules and support
Skill Gap: Learn Budget Management	Research workshops or courses in budget management	Jun 1, 2024	Jun 30, 2024	Online search tools, professional network
	Attend workshop or course	Jul 1, 2024	Aug 15, 2024	Workshop materials, budget
	Apply skills in a work-place project	Oct 1, 2024	Ongoing	Internal team, supervisor
Overall Goal: Apply for Office Manager Position	Update résumé to emphasise skills and experience	Jul 1, 2024	Jul 30, 2024	Résumé templates, LinkedIn profile

	Update LinkedIn Profile to reflect new skills and certifications	Aug 1, 2024	Aug 15, 2024	LinkedIn Profile
	Apply for 2 internal positions	Sep 1, 2024	Sep 30, 2024	Company online job board
	Apply for 2 external positions	Oct 1, 2024	Oct 31, 2024	External job platforms
	Network with colleagues who are office managers	*Nov 1, 2024*	Ongoing	Internal team, professional network
Overall Goal: Seek Feedback and Mentorship	Initiate regular meetings with mentor	Oct 1, 2024	Ongoing	Schedule of monthly meetings with a mentor
	Seek feedback from colleagues and super-visors	Oct 1, 2024	Ongoing	Internal team, supervisor

Extra columns can be added for additional notes and updates.

This example demonstrates the use of a structured action plan that utilises **SMART goals** and addresses **skill gaps** in order to pursue a career advancement goal.

- **Specific**: Each action step is clearly defined.
- **Measurable**: Progress is tracked by completed enrolments, certifications, updated documents, and feedback.
- **Achievable**: Goals are realistic and broken down into manageable tasks.
- **Relevant**: Actions are aligned with the career goal of transitioning from Administrative Assistant to Office Manager.
- **Time-bound**: Deadlines are set for each step, ensuring progress stays on track.

This table also includes space to describe **resources needed** and a method to **track progress** which are key elements of a comprehensive action plan as discussed in our conversation. The action steps include elements of both **skill development** and also **strategic networking**. The plan can be easily tracked using a simple spreadsheet or project management software, which were also discussed in our previous conversation.

Conclusion

Well done! You've done the hard work. This chapter was dedicated to transforming your insights from self-assessment and research into a concrete, comprehensive career action plan. By bringing together your goals, skills, and opportunities, you've created a powerful document that will serve as your blueprint for professional growth. This plan is not just a collection of tasks; it is a declaration of your professional intent and a strategic tool for navigating your career. But a plan, no matter how detailed, is only as effective as your commitment to it. In the next chapter, we'll cover the crucial final step: monitoring and adjusting your plan to ensure it remains a dynamic and effective road map for your professional journey.

CHAPTER 11

Step 7: Monitoring and Adjusting Your Plan

In the previous chapter, we successfully completed **Step 6** of the career planning process, building a detailed and comprehensive action plan. We used a structured approach to translate your aspirations into a tangible document, complete with actionable steps, timelines, and resources. Now, we're ready for one final and ongoing step—**Step 7: Monitoring and Adjusting Your Career Action Plan**.

This process is what transforms your plan from a static document into a dynamic and flexible road map for your professional journey. It ensures you stay on track, adapt to challenges, and continue moving toward your goals. There are several key reasons why this step is so important:

- **Track Progress**: Regular check-ins let you see what's working and what isn't, keeping you on the right path.
- **Adapt to Changes**: The job market and your personal life are always evolving. Adjusting your plan allows you to pivot and adapt to new opportunities or unexpected challenges.
- **Stay Motivated**: Seeing tangible progress—even small wins—boosts your morale and helps you stay motivated.
- **Identify Obstacles**: Proactive monitoring helps you spot obstacles early so you can address them before they derail your progress.
- **Continuous Improvement**: This process fosters a mindset of ongoing growth, encouraging you to refine your skills and strategies for better outcomes.
- **Ensure Alignment**: As you grow and change, your goals may too. Adjusting your plan ensures it remains aligned with your current aspirations and values.

In this chapter, we will go through the practical steps of how to monitor and adjust your career action plan effectively.

Steps in Monitoring and Adjusting Your Career Action Plan
1. Set Milestones and Review Timelines

Start by breaking your larger career goals into smaller, manageable milestones that serve as checkpoints. These can be short-term (monthly) or long-term (quarterly or annually). Establish regular review periods to assess your progress and evaluate what you've achieved so far.

2. Track Your Progress

Use specific metrics to track your progress, such as the number of new skills acquired or projects completed. Use tools like spreadsheets, career management software, or apps to log your achievements and deadlines. Keeping a journal can also be valuable for documenting successes, challenges, and lessons learned, providing a clear picture of your journey.

3. Evaluate Current Strategies

Regularly ask yourself whether your current actions are helping you reach your goals. Seek feedback from mentors, peers, or supervisors to gain different perspectives on your progress and to identify areas for improvement. Use this feedback to make necessary adjustments to your plan.

4. Identify Obstacles and Challenges

Be honest with yourself about any barriers that are holding you back. These could be related to a skill gap, a lack of resources, or a personal challenge. Understand the root causes of these obstacles so you can develop effective solutions.

5. Adapt and Modify Goals

Your goals may evolve as you grow, and that's okay. Be flexible and ready to adjust your goals, timelines, or strategies based on new insights or changes in your circumstances. This could mean setting new targets or changing your approach entirely.

6. Develop New Skills

Continuously assess what skills are necessary for your career path. Stay updated on industry trends and technologies by pursuing learning opportunities like courses, workshops, or seminars to acquire the skills you need.

7. Reinforce Motivation

Acknowledge and celebrate your achievements, no matter how small, to boost morale and maintain a positive mindset. Remember to also revisit your "why"—the reasons you set your career goals in the first place—to rekindle your purpose and inspiration.

Accountability: The Glue That Binds Commitment to Results

As Bob Proctor (Proctor, n.d.) famously said, "accountability is the glue that ties commitment to the result." Accountability is essential for turning intentions into actions and ensuring you make consistent progress. It is the key to staying focused on your goals and building momentum.

Here are some strategies to enhance your accountability:

- **Set Clear, SMART Goals:** Begin by defining your goals using the **SMART** framework. Instead of a general goal like "get a better job," set a specific goal like, "I will apply to five project management positions per week."

- **Create a Detailed Timeline:** Break down your goals into smaller, more manageable tasks with clear deadlines to prevent procrastination. For instance, "complete the project management course by September 2025."
- **Find an Accountability Partner:** Share your goals with a trusted friend, mentor, or colleague who can provide support, encouragement, and constructive feedback. This person will help keep you on track.
- **Schedule Regular Check-ins:** Plan regular meetings with your accountability partner to discuss progress, challenges, and next steps. These meetings provide a structured opportunity to address any roadblocks.
- **Leverage Technology:** Use apps and tools like Trello, Asana, or simple calendar reminders to track your tasks and deadlines.
- **Document Your Progress:** Keep a journal or log of your achievements and setbacks. Reflecting on your journey can be highly motivating and help you learn from your experiences.
- **Reward Yourself for Achievements:** Celebrate both small and large victories. Rewards boost morale and help sustain motivation throughout the process.
- **Maintain Flexibility:** Be ready to adapt your plan if unexpected challenges arise. Flexibility ensures you can stay on course without becoming discouraged.
- **Seek Feedback from Peers and Mentors:** Regularly ask for constructive criticism to gain new insights and refine your approach.
- **Cultivate a Positive Mindset:** Believe in your ability to reach your goals. A positive attitude enhances resilience and helps you persevere, even when faced with difficulties.

Additional Insights on Consistency

- **The Two-Day Rule:** The "Two-Day Rule" is a core concept in Matt D'Avella's work on habit formation and productivity. He discusses it in his YouTube videos, and a course titled Simple Habits (D'avella, 2019). D'avella suggests following your goals daily without skipping more than two days in a row. This approach helps you maintain momentum. If you miss a day, just get back on track the next day.
- **Persistence:** Remember that achieving success requires consistent effort and dedication. It's important to show up and put in the workday after day, even when you don't feel like it.

By actively employing these strategies, you can reinforce your commitment, stay motivated, and ensure your career action plan remains a living tool that guides you effectively through your professional journey. Remember, flexibility and adaptability are key to thriving in today's dynamic work environments.

CHAPTER 12

Continuous Learning and Professional Relationships

Bonus Step 8

In the previous chapter, we mastered the crucial final step of career planning: monitoring and adjusting our road map. Now, as we have identified new goals and potential gaps, we turn to two very powerful tools for executing those adjustments: **continuous learning** and building strong **professional relationships**. These are not optional elements for success—they are the dynamic forces that propel you forward in a career that is constantly in motion, ensuring your plan remains a living, powerful road map.

The Importance of Continuous Learning and Adaptability

In a rapidly evolving professional landscape, your greatest asset is your ability to evolve. **Continuous learning** is the proactive, lifelong pursuit of knowledge and skill development to maintain your professional relevance. It's the engine that keeps you moving, ensuring you remain competitive and capable of tackling new challenges.

By proactively seeking out new information, technologies, and best practises, you don't just stay current—you get ahead of the curve. This commitment to ongoing learning enhances your job performance, boosts your value to employers, and unlocks new career opportunities that a static skill set could never access.

Adaptability is the result of this continuous learning. It is the ability to adjust to new conditions and embrace change as an opportunity for growth. Instead of viewing change with apprehension, you learn to see it as a chance to enhance your problem-solving abilities and foster a mindset of innovation.

Forging Your Professional Ecosystem: Networking and Building Relationships

Networking is not about collecting contacts; it's about forging a **professional ecosystem** of genuine relationships that can fuel your career. This network provides a vital source of new opportunities, valuable referrals, and critical industry insights that are often inaccessible otherwise.

Strategies for Building Your Network:

- **Engage in Industry Events:** Actively participate in conferences, seminars, and workshops. Don't just attend; introduce yourself to speakers and peers and ask meaningful questions.
- **Join Professional Associations:** Becoming a member of a relevant organisation instantly connects you to a community of like-minded professionals. Volunteer for a committee or leadership role to get more deeply involved.
- **Utilise Online Platforms:** Leverage platforms like LinkedIn to connect with colleagues and thought leaders. Engage with their content and share your own insights to build a credible online presence.
- **Conduct Informational Interviews:** Strategically reach out to professionals in your field for a brief chat to gain advice and insights. This is a direct, respectful way to learn and build a genuine connection.

Fostering Your Relationships:

Your network is built on reciprocity. Focus on giving as much as you receive. Be genuine in your interactions, offer assistance, and share valuable resources. Always **follow up** after meetings and make a conscious effort to stay connected and nurture your relationships over time.

Developing Your Continuous Learning and Networking Action Plan

To make continuous learning and networking a habit, you need to treat it like a project. Here is a structured approach to developing your own action plan.

1. **Conduct Your Personal Skills Audit:** Begin by taking an honest look at your current skills and passions. Utilise tools like skills inventories, personality assessments, or a simple SWOT analysis to understand your strengths and weaknesses. This step directly connects to the skills gap analysis we conducted in a previous chapter, helping you identify what you need to learn next.
2. **Define Your Learning and Networking Objectives:**
    - **Short-Term Goals:** Set specific, measurable learning goals for the next year (e.g., "Complete a data analytics certification").
    - **Long-Term Goals:** Define where you want your career to be in 3-5 years and identify the skills and relationships you'll need to get there.
3. **Identify Learning and Networking Opportunities:** Research relevant courses, certifications, workshops, and seminars. Explore mentorship programs and make a list of key indi-

viduals or groups you want to connect with. Make it a habit to read industry-related books, articles, and newsletters.

4. **Create Your Action Timeline:** Develop a timeline for each step of your plan. This includes setting deadlines for completing courses, attending events, or reaching out to new contacts. List all the resources you require to achieve your goals.
5. **Review, Adapt, and Get Feedback:** Regularly document your achievements, analyse what worked and what didn't, and be prepared to adjust your plan as necessary. Most importantly, actively seek feedback from mentors and peers. They can provide invaluable guidance and help you course-correct when needed.

Example Format: Continuous Learning Action Plan

The following illustrate how you can develop a continuous learning plan using a tabular format:

Component	Details
Name:	[Your Name]
Date:	[Start Date]
Review Date:	[Periodic Review Date]
1. Skills Assessment	Current Skills: [List your current skills]
	Areas for Improvement: [Identify skills to develop]
2. Objectives	Short-Term Goals: [Define goals for the upcoming year]
	Long-Term Goals: [Define goals for the next 3-5 years]
3. Learning Opportunities	Courses/Certifications: [List potential courses and institutions]
	Workshops/Seminars: [Identify upcoming events]
	Mentoring Opportunities: [Name potential mentors or coaching programs]

	Online Learning Platforms: [Explore available courses]
4. Networking Strategies	Target Individuals/Groups: [Identify key people/groups to connect with]
	Monthly Networking Goals: [Set monthly targets for networking activities]
	Follow-Up Plan: [Outline regular follow-up actions]
5. Action Plan	Timeline: [Create a timeline for the steps to be taken]
	Resources Needed: [List required resources]
6. Review & Feedback	Progress Notes: [Record achievements and insights]
	Adjustments: [Note any plan modifications]

The Mindset of a Proactive Professional

Continuous learning and effective networking are not just a set of actions; they are a direct result of cultivating the right mindset. This proactive approach is rooted in the principles we explored in early chapters, particularly the importance of intentional thinking and embracing a growth mindset.

- From Intentionality to Proactiveness: In earlier chapters, we defined intentionality as the conscious alignment of your actions with your goals. Here, we apply this by moving beyond simply reacting to job market shifts. A proactive mindset means you are constantly looking ahead—identifying future skill needs and building relationships before you need them. It's about taking ownership of your career and anticipating challenges, rather than waiting for them to happen.
- Embracing a Growth Mindset: The foundation of continuous learning is a growth mindset—the belief that your abilities can be developed through dedication and hard work. This is the opposite of a fixed mindset, which assumes your talents are static. By embracing a growth mindset, you view every challenge as an opportunity to learn, every setback as a chance to grow, and every new skill as a pathway to greater professional fulfilment. This mindset turns the "how-to" steps of this chapter into a natural and rewarding part of your journey.

By consciously adopting this proactive, growth-oriented mindset, you empower yourself to not only follow the steps in your plan but to continuously shape and refine your career path.

Common Pitfalls and How to Overcome Them

Even with the best intentions, professionals often encounter obstacles in their continuous learning and networking journeys. Being aware of these common pitfalls is the first step toward avoiding them.

Pitfalls of Continuous Learning

- **The "Knowledge Hoarding" Trap:** A common mistake is to endlessly consume courses, books, and articles without ever applying the new knowledge. This leads to a false sense of progress. To overcome this, implement a **"Learn-and-Apply" rule**. For every new concept you learn, immediately find a way to apply it to your current work, a personal project, or a mock scenario. This solidifies the knowledge and proves its value.
- **The "Shiny Object Syndrome":** Getting distracted by every new trend or technology can pull your focus in too many directions, preventing you from mastering a single, valuable skill. It is important to stick to your plan. Revisit the skills you identified in your action plan and commit to them. Only after you've made significant progress should you consider a new learning path.

Pitfalls of Professional Networking

- **Networking for Personal Gain Only:** Approaching relationships with a transactional mindset—only reaching out when you need something—is a sure way to alienate your network. It is best to adopt a **"Give-First" mentality**. Make it a habit to offer help, share valuable insights, or make connections for others without expecting anything in return. These builds trust and strengthen your reputation.
- **The Fear of Rejection:** Many professionals hesitate to reach out to influential people or attend events alone for fear of being rejected or feeling out of place. Instead, start small and redefine your goal. Instead of trying to meet "important" people, aim to have one meaningful conversation with a person you find interesting. This lowers the pressure and makes networking more approachable.

Harnessing Collective Wisdom: The Power of Mastermind Groups and Believing Partners

You don't have to navigate these challenges alone. Overcoming many of these pitfalls is far easier with the right support system.

- **Mastermind Groups:** A mastermind group is a small, dedicated group of peers who meet regularly to help each other solve problems and achieve goals. Tapping into the benefits of **collective thinking** provides diverse perspectives, holds you accountable, and helps you overcome mental blocks. In these groups, your peers serve as a sounding board, offering honest feedback and innovative solutions that you might not have considered on your own.
- **Partners in Believing:** These are key individuals in your life who support your career aspirations even when you feel like giving up on your dreams. A "partner in believing" could be a mentor, a close friend, or a family member. They are the ones who remind you of your "why," celebrate your small victories, and provide the encouragement you need to persevere through setbacks. Cultivating these relationships is crucial for maintaining the motivation required for long-term growth and success.

Conclusion

Continuous learning and building professional relationships are not just tasks to check off a list; they are foundational to a thriving career. As we've seen, embracing a proactive mindset—one rooted in intentionality and a growth mindset—is what transforms these activities into a powerful, lifelong strategy. By actively seeking out new knowledge and forging genuine connections, you are not just keeping up with the world; you are positioning yourself to lead.

The journey won't be without its challenges. You may face the "shiny object syndrome" or the fear of rejection, but these are no match for a strategic approach. By recognising common pitfalls and proactively surrounding yourself with mastermind groups and partners in believing, you build a resilient support system. This network provides the accountability, collective wisdom, and unwavering support you need to persevere through setbacks and realise your full potential.

Ultimately, your commitment to learning and your network of relationships will be your greatest assets. They are the keys to sustained professional relevance, personal growth, and the confidence to not only reach your goals but to continuously create new ones.

SECTION THREE

THE ENTREPRENEURIAL MINDSET

CHAPTER 13

Navigating the Global Employment Maze

Converting Credentials into Currency

This section is your blueprint for escaping the limitations of the traditional job market. We aim to spark your vision for an independent, resilient future, where you transform from a skilled job seeker into a dynamic opportunity creator. For those already on their journey and feeling stuck, remember it is never too late to start dreaming and to pivot to align with your dreams.

The Global Reality: A Structural Problem, Not a Personal Failure

If you are a professional grappling with underemployment, rest assured that this is often a structural issue, not a reflection of your worth or capability. Global trends show persistent challenges that disproportionately affect skilled populations in developing economies:

Youth Unemployment: Globally, the youth unemployment rate stood at 13% in 2023, which is significantly higher than the adult rate of around 5% (ILO, 2024). This disparity highlights a structural blockage where new talent cannot enter the formal workforce, leading to high levels of anxiety among young people (ILO, 2024).

Informal Sector Dominance: Approximately 2 billion workers are in informal employment worldwide, accounting for around 58% of the global workforce (ILO, 2024). While providing income, this reality highlights a lack of social protection and job security, often forcing skilled professionals into roles that do not fully utilise their education.

Underemployment Crisis (The Jobs Gap): Beyond outright joblessness, the total number of persons without employment who are interested in finding a job—known as the global "jobs gap"—reached 402 million persons in 2024 (ILO, 2024). This figure measures the pervasive issue of labour underutilisation and underemployment—workers who are working reduced hours or holding positions well below their educational and skill level.

Consider the reality of Trudy, a highly skilled professional in the health field in Jamaica. Despite over 20 years of experience, she felt stuck in the same junior role for over a decade. She had done every possible upskilling course, applied for every opportunity, and was repeatedly told she was "next in line." The harsh reality was that there were few senior roles and too many experienced candidates. When opportunities did materialise, Trudy noted that several male colleagues who had joined the workforce 5 to 15 years after her were consistently prioritised for acting appointments and senior roles. This systemic blockage and perceived gender bias left Trudy so discouraged and disenfranchised that she stopped applying altogether, now viewing her job as merely "honouring the profession" and going through the motions. Trudy's story perfectly illustrates the depth of the structural mismatch—it is a soul-crushing problem that stems from a lack of market capacity, not a lack of effort.

The Migration Paradox: When Opportunity Becomes Underemployment

The issue of skilled workers facing job stagnation or unemployment is a global concern, but the complexities intensify when highly skilled individuals migrate overseas in search of opportunity. The transition is often far from smooth, particularly in destinations like Australia.

In the Australian context, many highly skilled African migrants, despite possessing tertiary qualifications, frequently find their human resources "underutilised" due to the lack of acknowledgement of their professional qualifications by employers (Robinson, Afrouz, & Dunwoodie, 2025). Highly experienced individuals often find themselves employed in lower-paid positions than what they were qualified for (Fisher, 2013; Robinson, Afrouz, & Dunwoodie, 2025).

My personal story began as a highly skilled, senior-level Environmental Health professional migrating from Jamaica to Australia. Armed with extensive experience, I applied for numerous Environmental Health Officer roles, yet my applications often vanished, yielding little response from recruiters. It was a deeply discouraging experience. I later discovered the painful truth: because my qualifications were not conferred by an accredited Australian institution, my credentials required mandatory assessment before I could practice in my field. Despite submitting countless applications, this crucial prerequisite was never highlighted by recruiters—a process I only uncovered later through internal experience within the health system.

This experience of **professional invisibility** is tragically common among migrant professionals. For many, the journey involves acute challenges in finding suitable employment, often leading to underemployment or forced career changes. Highly qualified individuals—including medical professionals, engineers, educators, medical scientists, and legal professionals—some with decades of service in mid-level and senior roles in their home countries—face rejection or are asked to retrain. The barriers are structural and systemic, including the lack of acknowledgement of professional qualifications by employers, the high costs and complexity of recognising overseas qualifications, or factors as subtle as recruiters disliking their accent or perceiving they do not **"look like"** or would not be **"a good fit"** for the role.

Through hosting the *My Career My Calling* podcast, I have interviewed numerous migrant professionals who share similar stories of resilience and struggle. The journey demands perseverance, a willingness to adopt unconventional strategies, and immense determination:

- One professional, possessing a Master's degree in Finance, detailed the struggle to bypass barriers against international students applying for graduate roles. He strategically applied for a low-level position in a bank's mail room (posting letters), viewing it as the critical first step to get his **"foot in the door"** and gain local access to systems and networks necessary to climb the corporate ladder.

- Another interviewee recounted a friend, a doctor from Africa, who, unable to secure a medical position, became creative: he reframed his skills and applied for a non-existent role as an **"assistant in the theater"** in Western Australia to secure initial health system experience.

- A drama teacher, determined not to settle for unrelated work like aged care, took a job as a cleaner in a private drama school just to be physically present in the desired professional environment. The principal reviewed her CV, which showcased her actual teaching skills, leading quickly to a part-time teaching role and eventually establishing her as a top drama teacher.

These stories underscore that the struggle is real, but so too is the capacity for resilience and success among migrant professionals who refuse to give up on their dreams. Accepting these jobs is often viewed as a necessary step to gain local experience and get a "foot in the door." However, the difficulty in finding employment commensurate with overseas qualifications is compounded by the fact that these qualifications may not readily integrate with the Australian system, potentially requiring immigrants to pursue retraining or local accreditation. Data consistently shows that recently arrived migrants face barriers to inclusion and integration, particularly in employment, and often face higher unemployment rates than established residents.

"It was a deeply discouraging experience. I later discovered the painful truth: because my qualifications were not conferred by an accredited Australian institution, my credentials required mandatory assessment before I could practice in my field. Despite submitting countless applications, this crucial prerequisite was never highlighted by recruiters—a process I only uncovered later through internal experience within the health system."

This structural mismatch has significant social and economic consequences. Women, specifically, have struggled to find work in their respective fields despite their tertiary qualifications (Robinson, Afrouz, & Dunwoodie, 2025). For men, facing unemployment or underemployment is especially challenging, as they may have previously occupied a higher status as the head of the household (Fisher, 2013; Robinson, Afrouz, & Dunwoodie, 2025). This shift directly impacts family dynamics and economic stability (Fisher, 2013; Robinson, Afrouz, & Dunwoodie, 2025). Furthermore, **financial instability** often prevents women from exercising their legal rights when facing Domestic and Family Violence (DFV), increasing their feelings of isolation and jeopardising their autonomy (Vasil, 2023; Robinson, Afrouz, & Dunwoodie, 2025).

Accepting these jobs is often viewed as a necessary step to gain local experience and get a "foot in the door." However, the difficulty in finding employment commensurate with overseas qualifications is compounded by the fact that these qualifications may not readily integrate with the Australian system, potentially requiring immigrants to pursue retraining or local accreditation. Data consistently shows that recently arrived migrants face barriers to inclusion and integration, particularly in employment, and often face higher unemployment rates than established residents.

The core challenge is a structural mismatch. Developing nations often struggle with a capital deficit that prevents the creation of enough formal, high-value jobs to match a growing, educated labour force. Furthermore, rapid technological advancements, like automation and AI, create structural unemployment, making older job roles obsolete faster than new ones are created.

The Core Challenge: Structural Barriers vs. Transferable Value

For professionals who have invested heavily in education (like public health experts), this structural problem demands a strategic response. If the formal sector cannot absorb your credentials, you must pivot to creating your own demand.

The solution lies in two powerful, interconnected steps:

- Acknowledge Your Assets: Revisit the work you did in the previous chapters on Self-Reflection and Skills Assessment. Your academic history and professional training have equipped you with high-value transferable skills—analytical thinking, research rigour, complex problem-solving, and communication. These skills are your true currency.

- Define the Pivot: You must shift your identity from being an Employment Seeker (waiting for a vacancy to be posted) to an Opportunity Creator (identifying needs and delivering solutions).

The traditional path relies on external infrastructure (job market). The transformative path relies on internal assets (your skills and vision) to build your own infrastructure.

Sometimes, the structural barriers are amplified by personal circumstances. Here is a hypothetical example.

Consider Marlon, who originated from West Africa and undertook both undergraduate and postgraduate studies overseas. Tradition dictated that he was responsible for supporting his family back home. This relentless pressure forced him to forgo a crucial, unpaid internship opportunity—despite graduating with high distinction—so he could keep working and sending money home. Though academically brilliant, Marlon lacked the practical, hands-on experience employers sought and struggled in interviews. His high-distinction degree could not overcome the experience gap, a gap created not by choice, but by the financial demands of a broader social structure.

Navigating Pressure: Resilience and the Pivot

Marlon's experience clearly illustrates a critical challenge: the inability to invest in one's career due to overwhelming societal or family pressures. This forced trade-off between immediate survival (sending money home) and long-term career growth (gaining experience) poses a significant challenge, risking job stagnation or underemployment. To navigate this:

Set Boundaries and Communicate: Professionals must learn the vital skill of setting boundaries. Marlon needed to establish clear communication and financial expectations with his family, framing the internship not as a failure to provide, but as a high-return investment that would exponentially increase his future earning potential. This protects your time and energy, viewing professional development as a critical asset, not a negotiable burden.

Adopt a Growth Mindset and Develop Resilience: When facing setbacks, such as repeated interview failures or the inability to take an internship, embracing a growth mindset is crucial. View rejection not as a final judgement on your competence, but as vital data. This fosters a resilient approach to overcome setbacks, prompting you to seek smaller, project-based volunteer roles or short-term contracts that mimic the experience you missed, allowing you to bridge the gap strategically.

Understanding When to Pivot: The point where persistent societal pressure consistently thwarts your traditional career path is the signal to pivot. For Marlon, this meant recognising that the cost of meeting his family's traditional expectations prevented him from satisfying the market's requirements. This realisation—that the system is fundamentally blocked for your current circumstances—is the call to action to move from being an Employment Seeker to an Opportunity Creator.

Beyond Conformity: The Power of a Vision-Driven Career

Marlon's struggle is amplified by a widespread cultural pressure, particularly in developing contexts, to conform to traditional, seemingly secure professions (doctor, lawyer, nurse, accountant). While these careers are honourable, the modern, globalised economy—coupled with local structural deficits—demands that you seek value over title.

The key to overcoming professional stagnation is to cast a vision early in one's career journey. This involves shifting the focus from simply meeting familial or societal expectations to identifying one's true purpose, passions, and core values. When career decisions are driven by personal vision, they naturally steer young people toward professions or skilled roles that maximise their potential impact and profitability.

This intentional approach requires parental and educational partnership. Parents and educators must guide students preparing to leave high school to look beyond the college degree track. Success can be found in vocational trades, specialised apprenticeships, and technical training that set the foundation for a thriving business, turning a skilled trade into an entrepreneurial venture, an invention, or community leadership. The possibilities truly are endless when a career is approached with a vision-driven mindset.

Despite the often-dismal unemployment rates and professional barriers, immense possibilities exist for those who are intentional about their vocational pathways. Readers, especially those facing limited opportunities and lacking clarity on their next steps, can tap into the information provided here and in the subsequent chapters on the Entrepreneurial Mindset to effectively overcome the unemployment and professional progression slump.

The Way Forward: Leveraging Digital Tools and Micro-Enterprises

For those already on their journeys and feeling stuck, it is never too late to start dreaming and to pivot to align with their dreams. Instead of viewing the limited local market as a barrier, view it as a competitive landscape where only the most adaptable will thrive. The solution involves directly monetising your high-value skills by leveraging global digital platforms and local resources.

1. Monetising Skills in the Digital Arena (The Gig Economy)

The internet is borderless and provides an immediate solution to the structural unemployment caused by local capital deficits.

Gig Work and E-commerce: Platforms allow you to offer high-level services (research, writing, data analysis, consulting) directly to global clients. You can immediately monetise your transferable skills without waiting for a local job opening. Furthermore, you can leverage e-commerce platforms to sell local goods or knowledge-based products (e-books, courses, templates).

AI-Enhanced Productivity: Free, accessible tools like Gemini 2.5 Flash and other generative AI platforms are game-changers. They allow individuals to drastically boost productivity in service-related tasks, essentially acting as a digital workforce without requiring massive capital investment. This levels the playing field, making one skilled professional as productive as a small team.

Digital Skills Training: Online courses and digital public goods initiatives (like DIKSHA) offer accessible, scalable training. They help you bridge any skill gaps created by technological change, ensuring your knowledge base remains current and competitive.

2. Harnessing Local Resources (Micro-Enterprise & Local Impact)

The second path involves identifying and filling local service gaps that larger, formal businesses overlook.

Micro-enterprises: Start small businesses utilising readily available local resources, knowledge, or creative talents. This could involve specialised consulting, local training, or creating unique, value-added products that meet a local need. Specific examples include professional coaching, book writing, tutoring, professional editing, language interpretation, translation of documents, and creating local solutions to importation challenges by developing value-added services.

Knowledge & Creativity: Your professional experience is valuable content. Monetise your unique knowledge by creating content, podcasts, or offering specialised training services that solve specific community or organisational problems.

Embracing the Creator Mindset

Unemployment and underemployment are challenging realities, but they are not the end of your professional narrative. They are an urgent invitation to embrace a different model—one where you are the primary investor in your career.

The hypothetical story of Janice encapsulates this pivot perfectly.

Janice, a highly skilled teacher with a flair for business strategy, who is creative and has an active imagination, left her job after experiencing workplace issues. Despite multiple unsuccessful attempts to return to the formal workforce, she remained resolute. During her absence, she began creating and selling art to locals. She then started writing books about her experiences and other topics of interest, eventually launching an online community. Over time, she developed momentum and now generates multiple streams of income through partnerships and value-added online services, completely bypassing the need for traditional employment in her original field.

By revisiting your transferable skills, leveraging global digital platforms, and focusing on creating value, you bypass the bottleneck of the formal job market.

This pivot requires more than just action; it requires a complete Entrepreneurial Mindset. The next chapter will provide you with the framework to cultivate this mindset, transforming you from a skilled job seeker into a dynamic opportunity creator.

CHAPTER 14

The Entrepreneurial Mindset:

Leveraging Your Skills to Start Your Own Business

Transitioning from a traditional career path to entrepreneurship requires a shift in mindset. This chapter will guide you through the key mental frameworks necessary to leverage your professional and transferable skills to start and grow a successful business, drawing on the principles of growth, resilience, and strategic action.

Cultivating a Growth Mindset

- **Challenges as Opportunities:** A core component of an entrepreneurial mindset is viewing challenges as opportunities for growth. Rather than seeing obstacles as roadblocks, view them as chances to innovate, learn, and adapt. This perspective transforms difficulties into stepping stones
- **Belief in Development:** Embrace the idea that your abilities can be developed through dedication and hard work. This belief is essential for breaking free from limiting beliefs and pushing toward your goals.
- **Gratitude and Positivity**: Practise gratitude daily to maintain a positive outlook, which is crucial for navigating the ups and downs of entrepreneurship. This positive attitude can help you overcome self-doubt and stay motivated.
- **Overcoming Limiting Beliefs:** Identify and challenge the invisible chains of limiting beliefs that can hold you back from reaching your full potential. Replace thoughts like "I'm not capable" with empowering affirmations such as "With effort and perseverance, I can learn and succeed."

The Power of Vision and Intention

- **Clear Vision:** Develop a clear and compelling vision for your business. Without a vision, it's easy to wander aimlessly. Your vision provides a blueprint for your life, outlining your goals and aspirations.
- **Specificity:** Intentionality is the bridge between your vision and your actions. This requires specificity. Vague intentions yield vague results; therefore, you must be specific with your intentions. Instead of "I want to be successful," state, "I intend to launch a successful online business within the next year that generates $100,000 in revenue".
- **Written Plans:** Create a written plan that outlines your vision and strategies to achieve it. Consider the "12 buckets" approach, which represents key areas of your life, such as personal brand, relationships, and finances. For each bucket, set specific goals and intentions, creating a road map for intentional living.

- **Daily Alignment**: Translate your vision and strategy into daily activities. Your daily actions should be aligned with your goals and designed to move you closer to your desired outcomes. For example, if a goal is to write a book, your daily activities might include writing for a set amount of time each day.
- **Innovation and Resourcefulness**: Intentionality fuels innovation, pushing you to find solutions even when faced with limitations. Embrace a mindset of possibility, challenging limitations that hold you back from pursuing your dreams.

Resilience and Perseverance

- **Embrace Failure:** Understand that failure is not the opposite of success but a part of it. View setbacks as opportunities to learn and grow. Every challenge you overcome makes you stronger and more resilient.
- **Maintain Discipline:** Maintain discipline in your habits to ensure consistent progress. Set specific times for daily activities and stick to them (.
- **Stay Focused:** Focus on your goals and limit distractions by setting specific work hours and sticking to them.
- **Persistence:** Persist in the face of challenges. Set a specific time each day to work on challenging projects until they are complete. Consistency is key to reaching your destination.
- **Bounce Back:** Develop the resilience to bounce back from setbacks stronger. Reflect on past failures and write down the lessons learned.
- **Responsibility**: Take responsibility for your actions, rectifying mistakes to ensure integrity in your endeavours.

Leveraging Self-Belief

- **Believe in Your Potential:** Believe in your own potential and that your thoughts have the power to shape your reality. Write down affirmations about your strengths every morning to reinforce your self-belief.
- **Develop Confidence:** Develop and exude confidence. Practise speaking about your achievements in front of a mirror to build assurance.

Actionable Steps for Mindset Development

- **Start a Gratitude Journal:** Commit to writing in it daily to maintain a positive outlook.
- **Challenge Limiting Beliefs:** Identify a limiting belief and counter it with a positive, empowering affirmation.
- **Set Clear Goals:** Define your goals using the SMART framework, ensuring they are specific, measurable, achievable, relevant, and time bound.
- **Create a Detailed Action Plan**: Break down your goals into manageable tasks with timelines.

- **Commit to Daily Activities:** Dedicate a specific time each day to work on your goals, ensuring consistent progress.

Conclusion

Adopting an entrepreneurial mindset is the first step to launching your business. By combining a clear vision, a commitment to continuous learning, and a resilient attitude, you equip yourself with the necessary psychological foundation to achieve success. Remember that your mindset is the driving force that can turn aspirations into reality.

CHAPTER 15

Chapter 15: Building Your Business:

Skillset and Toolset for Success

In writing this book, I have drawn upon the wisdom and expertise of many thought leaders who have shaped my understanding of career development and personal growth. In particular, the principles shared by pioneers like Dean Graziosi, Anthony 'Tony' Robbins, Napoleon Hill, and Myron Golden have profoundly influenced my perspective. I have personally adapted and integrated many of their powerful teachings into the framework you will find within these pages, and I am grateful to be able to share what I have learned with you.

This chapter outlines the essential skills and tools needed to start and scale a knowledge-based business by leveraging your professional and transferable skills. Drawing from the principles of product innovation, revenue generation, and strategic planning, this chapter will guide you through practical steps to create a thriving business. This is not meant to be an exhaustive guide, but rather an introduction to possible next steps for skilled and experienced professionals who are seeking ideas for their next career transition.

Essential Skills for the Modern Entrepreneur

At the core of any thriving business is a set of essential skills that go beyond professional expertise. **Product innovation** is paramount; it's the continuous process of developing unique and valuable services or products that directly address your clients' needs. In a knowledge-based business, this means constantly refining your offerings to be as relevant and impactful as possible.

Beyond the product itself, you must master the art of **revenue generation**. This includes understanding sales and marketing to create an effective and compelling pathway for your clients to find and purchase your solution. Your ability to create an **irresistible offer** is key—it's not just about what you sell, but how you package it to solve your client's most pressing problem.

Strategic planning is the cornerstone of long-term success. It involves creating a clear vision for your goals and breaking it down into actionable steps. A crucial part of this is understanding how to be adaptable and resilient, allowing you to thrive even when market conditions are challenging.

Effective **time management** and **communication** are your personal productivity tools. By prioritising tasks and mastering active listening, you ensure your actions are always aligned with your goals and that your professional relationships are strong. Furthermore, sound **financial management** is non-negotiable, requiring you to implement systems for budgeting and tracking spending.

Continuous improvement is a non-negotiable part of the entrepreneurial journey. This includes fostering **creativity** in your problem-solving, seeking mentorship to gain guidance, and practising reflection on your daily experiences. Maintaining a **healthy lifestyle** is also essential, as your productivity and overall well-being are the foundations of your success. To maintain a healthy lifestyle, focus on planning your meals to ensure a balanced diet.

As an entrepreneur, your professional network is a valuable asset. **Networking** is crucial for gaining industry insights and building meaningful connections. Attend industry events and webinars to expand your network but remember that the goal is not just to collect contacts but to develop genuine relationships.

A mindset of **flexibility** and **curiosity** is also vital. Be open to new ideas and willing to change your routine if you discover a more efficient way of doing things. Stay curious and keep learning by watching documentaries or taking courses on topics you're unfamiliar with. This continuous learning will keep your skills and knowledge relevant in a constantly evolving market. Finally, the practice of **mindfulness** is a key skill. Being present in the moment can help you manage stress and improve focus. Set aside time for meditation or deep breathing exercises to cultivate this skill and maintain your overall well-being.

The Entrepreneurial Toolkit: Strategies and Practical Instruments

To execute these essential entrepreneurial skills, you need the right set of tools—both strategic and practical. Your journey begins with precise **Ideal Client Identification**. This is a critical first step that goes beyond demographics, focusing on understanding your target audience's core pain points and the specific solutions they are desperately seeking. By genuinely loving and serving your client, you can find a pathway to a solution that you offer, effectively bridging the gap between their current discontent and their desired future. This deep understanding informs your **Product Framework**, outlining the results you offer, your teaching topics, and your optimal delivery method.

Once you have clarity on your ideal client and product framework, you can develop an **Irresistible Offer**. A strong offer is the foundation of your brand and must clearly demonstrate how you help your clients achieve a specific result. Your offer should be so compelling that it meets their needs and gets them to fall in love with what you provide. This leads to effective **Product Development**, where you use your unique skills to create a service or product that delivers value. It is often best to start with one product, perfecting it with a process-oriented approach. This allows for continuous refinement as you share your work, recognising that both the product and your audience are perfecting it with you.

The **Sales Process** is the journey your client takes from discovering their need to receiving your solution. This journey begins with understanding that your client is experiencing discontent and desires a better life. To maximise their satisfaction, focus on decreasing the time between their payment and when they receive the value for their money. This swift delivery of value helps build trust and brand loyalty. Your **Marketing Strategies** should be a seamless blend of science and art. The science is in the delivery systems—the channels and platforms you use to reach your audience. The art is in the messaging—the creative, value-driven content you share to establish yourself as a thought leader. When you truly fall in love with your clients and deliver consistent value, they will fall in love with you in return.

Beyond these core business strategies, your toolkit for success includes practical instruments that support your operation. **Financial Tools** like a detailed budget and a spending tracker are essential for managing your finances wisely. **Planning Tools**—from digital apps to traditional planners—help you jot down tasks and manage deadlines efficiently. Leveraging **Technology** for online learning and other digital tools is also crucial to acquire new skills and expand your knowledge, keeping your business relevant and adaptable.

Taking Action: Your Road Map for Business Growth

The journey to building a thriving business is a continuous process of action and growth. To effectively navigate this path, consider these actionable steps:

- **Self-Reflection and Skills Assessment:** Begin by engaging in critical self-reflection. Examine your past experiences, accomplishments, and challenges to identify your unique strengths and weaknesses. This initial self-assessment is key to understanding what specific value you can offer in a business and forms the foundational step for effective product development.
- **Set SMART Goals:** Drive your business forward by setting SMART goals—goals that are Specific, Measurable, Achievable, Relevant, and Time-bound. Clearly defined goals provide direction and a framework for tracking your progress.
- **Commit to Continuous Learning:** In a dynamic market, committing to continuous learning is paramount to keeping your skills and knowledge relevant. Develop a **Continuous Learning Plan** that specifically identifies areas where you need to improve and strategies, practical ways to enhance those skills, ensuring you remain at the forefront of your field.
- **Create a Comprehensive Career Action Plan:** Develop a detailed plan that outlines your specific action steps, identifies necessary resources, sets realistic timelines, and establishes methods for tracking your progress. This plan serves as your personalised road map for business development.

- **Build and Nurture a Strong Network:** Recognise that you don't have to navigate the entrepreneurial journey alone. Actively create and nurture a professional network that supports your career growth. Your network can provide invaluable industry insights, collaboration opportunities, and emotional support.
- **Seek Mentorship:** Find a mentor who can guide you on your entrepreneurial journey. A mentor can offer expert advice, share experiences, and help you avoid common pitfalls, providing invaluable guidance and accelerating your growth.
- **Establish Accountability:** To stay on track and maintain momentum, find an accountability partner or enrol in a program. Having someone to report to or share your progress with can significantly increase your commitment and ensure you consistently take action towards your goals.

Conclusion

Starting a knowledge-based business requires a blend of specific skills and tools. By leveraging your unique strengths, focusing on product innovation, and strategically implementing the right tools, you can build a successful business that not only generates income but also creates a positive impact. Remember to always focus on your client and over-deliver on value. By developing the right mindset, skill set and tool set, you can launch and grow a business that leverages your professional and transferable skills.

Epilogue

Unleashing Your Dream Career

Congratulations! You've reached the end of **Beyond Limits: Manifesting and Unleashing Your Dream Career.**

As you began this journey, you were asked to design a career dream—a north star to guide you toward a professional life you'd love. This vision was never meant to be left on paper or treated as a mere goal. Instead, we have provided you with valuable tools and blueprints to make that dream tangible. Our hope is that you will use the action plan templates in this guide to create a meaningful, actionable plan and go forth to take small, consistent actions and maintain momentum toward achieving the career of your dreams.

This resource guide has not been a simple book to be read and set aside, but a comprehensive tool to be lived and implemented. As you turn these final pages, remember that you are not just closing a book—you are stepping into a new phase of your professional life, armed with the strategies and mindset to shape it on your own terms. We've journeyed from the deepest aspects of self-reflection to the most practical steps of execution, and this process has transformed your career aspirations from abstract ideas into a tangible, actionable reality. The principles and frameworks within these pages are designed to be your steadfast companions, providing guidance and clarity as you navigate the ever-evolving landscape of modern work.

The insights you have gained and the tools you have acquired are a testament to your commitment. This journey was never about finding a single, perfect job, but about understanding that your career is a dynamic, living entity that grows and adapts with you. It is about building a foundation of resilience and purpose that can withstand any challenge. From here on, your professional path is not a reaction to circumstance, but a deliberate creation born from your vision. You have moved beyond the traditional boundaries of career development and are now equipped to manifest a professional life that is not only successful but deeply fulfilling and aligned with your truest self.

A Recap of Your Journey
Section 1: The Foundation (Chapters 1-4)

We began by exploring the power of a vision-driven mindset in Chapter 1, teaching you how to design a dream for your career rooted in your purpose, passion, and core values. In Chapter 2, you learned to overcome the fears and self-limiting beliefs that often hold professionals back. We then moved to Chapter 3, which provided a comprehensive look at both internal and external barriers to career growth, and culminated in Chapter 4, where you learned to cultivate the resilience and growth mindset necessary to navigate any challenge.

Section 2: Career Action Planning (Chapters 5-12)

This is where your blueprint came to life. We started with the fundamentals of career planning in Chapter 5 and then dove into the 7-step career action plan. You learned to conduct a thorough skills assessment (Chapter 6), set SMART goals and research career options (Chapter 7), and identify and address skills gaps (Chapter 8). In Chapter 9, you discovered how to leverage your transferable skills for maximum impact. Finally, Chapters 10 and 11 guided you through the practical process of creating and continuously monitoring your comprehensive career action plan. Chapter 12 delved into the power of continuous learning and professional relationships, teaching you how to overcome common pitfalls and build a support system with mastermind groups and "partners in believing."

Sustaining Momentum Beyond Limits (Chapters 13-15)

In the final section, we equipped you with the tools for **long-term, sustained success**. The bonus chapters, Chapter 13 to Chapter 15 went **Beyond Limits** by showing you how to transcend the limitations of traditional employment. These chapters dive deep into how you can tap into your unique **skills, knowledge, and experience** to build a **thriving business** or **lucrative side-hustle**. This segment is especially valuable for those in their **mid-to-late career** who are looking for opportunities to leverage their lifetime of experience, pivot into something more impactful, and become their **own boss** to create true **time and financial freedom**.

The Path Forward

Now, the work truly begins. This book is a resource, and its true value lies in your engagement with it. The 7-step career action plan is intuitive and designed to be implemented at any stage of your career. It's a flexible framework that will grow with you.

We encourage you to use the templates in the appendices to start building your own vision-driven career today. Take the principles we've discussed and try them on. Find the grace and strength to pursue your dream, knowing that every hurdle is simply a test of your resolve. By consistently applying the strategies in this guide, you will not only overcome mindset-related challenges but will also foster a vision-driven growth mindset toward a more robust, impactful, and successful career.

As you step forward, remember that your career is a powerful extension of who you are. It is the canvas on which you will paint your impact on the world, a space where your unique talents and passions can come to life. The path may not always be straight, but with the map you've created, and a mustard seed sized faith, you have the clarity and confidence to navigate any turn. Use the templates, lean on your support system, and trust in the intentional work you have done to prepare for this journey.

Your dream career is not a destination to be reached, but a journey to be lived, and you now have the road map to unleash your full potential. Embrace it.

Endorsements

Dr. Fletcher-Lartey is truly an inspiration. She is multi-faceted, award winning, multi-talented, a woman of substance, with poise tenacity and humility. Her passion for teaching, sharing, mentoring and helping others to leverage their unrecognised transferable skills and using them to excel, has led to her launching her podcast on Career Development and now this in-depth book. An incredible resource for students from the high school level to the consummate professional, whether they are technical and vocational oriented, creative, entrepreneurial or the academically inclined.

This resource is valuable for personal development enrichment, career development programmes, human resource development and training, community and mentorship programmes and is not limited to a specific vocation, trade or career.

A must have for libraries, leaders, organisations and community development officers who participate in enrichment and mentoring programs. A very modern and relevant book for the 21st century, addressing relevant topics including entrepreneurship, diversity and artificial intelligence.

Lyssa-Ann Clarke – Trainer, Author, Publisher & Minister

The Creative Bizcoach & Leader of The Holistic Healing Ministries Jamaica

---

Beyond Limits: Manifesting and Unleashing Your Dream Career" is a timely and practical resource for anyone seeking clarity and growth in their professional journey. Dr. Stephanie Fletcher-Lartey has created more than a career guide—she has written a road map to professional fulfilment. Packed with wisdom and practical strategies, this book will empower readers to chart their path with clarity and conviction."

Pastor Emmanuel Adjei

Lead Pastor of FCI Sydney/ Councillor, Liverpool City Council, New South Wales Australia

---

"Dr. Stephanie Fletcher-Lartey's career transforming coaching is a daring movement indeed! _Beyond Limits_ is a break-over-the-wall, structured manual that walks beginners and middle-level professionals alike from the point of conception of career dreams to becoming impact makers in corporate and social workspace. This is a must study manual for career success."

Jon O. Attakora, President, Institute for Ethical Studies, Ghana

"It is with great joy and conviction that I endorse Beyond Limits: Manifesting and Unleashing Your Dreams Career by Dr. Stephenie Fletcher-Lartey. This book is not just another career guide, it is a timely, Spirit-inspired resource that empowers readers to rise above limitations, embrace divine purpose, and strategically plan their careers with excellence.

Dr. Fletcher-Lartey combines practical wisdom with a faith-filled perspective, offering a road map that will inspire, equip, and challenge you to discover your gifts, maximise your potential, and manifest the dreams God has placed in your heart. Whether you are a student, a young professional, or someone seeking a new direction in life, this book will ignite your passion, sharpen your vision, and position you for impact. I highly recommend this book to everyone who desires to live a life of significance beyond the ordinary. Beyond Limits is more than a guide, it is a catalyst for transformation."

Apostle Dr. Matthew Asemayina Dabu, Ph.D.

Lead Pastor, Anointed Truth and Life Ministries, Australia

"Beyond Limits: Manifesting and Unleashing Your Dream Career" is a powerful and practical guide for anyone seeking clarity, direction, and fulfilment in their career journey. Having had the privilege of being coached by Dr. Stephanie Fletcher-Lartey through her Dream Building Transformation Program, I have personally experienced how her insights inspire growth and empower change.

With over 15 years of service in the public sector, I found her approach invaluable in strengthening the soft and transferable skills that leaders and managers need to navigate challenges, lead teams, and deliver results. This book goes further—it offers a structured framework that is relevant not only for those advancing in established careers but also for those exploring new opportunities in consultancy, freelancing, or entrepreneurial ventures after leaving formal service.

Dr. Stephanie's wisdom and practical strategies provide a road map to help professionals at any stage embrace purpose, resilience, and continuous growth. This book is an essential companion for anyone ready to step beyond limits and unlock their dream career."

Loretta Ta'ake Whitney
Director for Children
Ministry of Women, Youth, Children & Family Affairs, Solomon Islands

It is an honour to endorse Dr. Stephanie Fletcher-Lartey's book, 'Beyond Limits: Manifesting and Unleashing Your Dream Career.'

Beyond Limits is more than a career book, it's an inspirational road map to personal and professional transformation.

With insights, wisdom and clarity, it empowers readers to believe in themselves, break barriers, and manifest the career they've always desired. It's a life-changing resource for dreamers and doers alike

Jennifer Richards Wilson

Activate Core

Other Books by Stephanie Fletcher-Lartey

THE PROFESSIONAL BELIEVER'S GUIDE: Principles To Help Christian Believers Thrive In The Market Place.

The Practice of Journaling Prayer, Testimony, and Gratitude: Expanded Edition
Stephanie M. Fletcher-Lartey

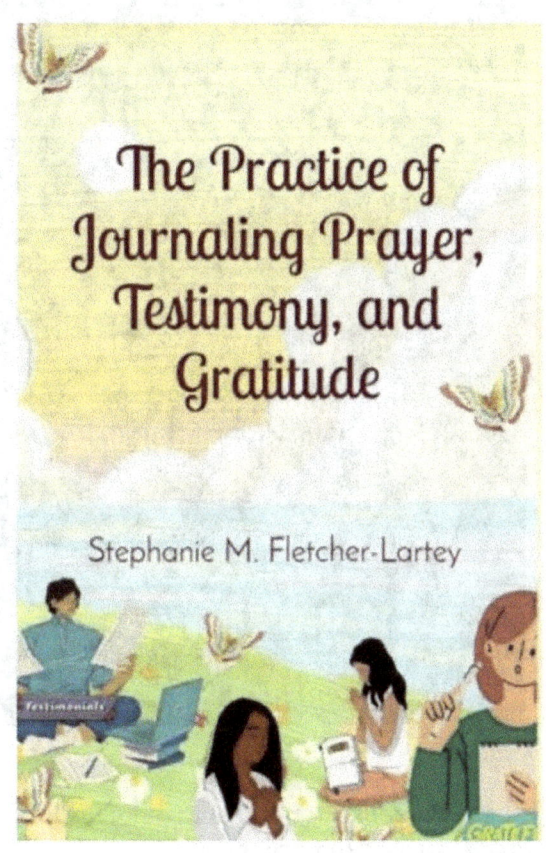

The Practice of Journaling Prayer, Testimony, and Gratitude: Expanded Edition
Stephanie M. Fletcher-Lartey

Co-authored this anthology with Kelly Markey

Echoes of Humanity: Exploring Human Wonders Through the Pages of: Lessons, Affliction, Triumph, Victory and Brilliance

Dr. Stephanie Fletcher – Lartey's books are available online. Please see Amazon link below: https://www.amazon.com/stores/author/B0D7T99SCK

Connect with Dr. Stephanie: Your Next Step Towards Purpose

Review Request

Thank you for reading! If you enjoyed this book, please consider leaving an honest review. It helps other readers discover it and supports my work as an author.

Thank you for choosing this book as your guide to transforming your career. Your journey doesn't end here—it's just beginning!

To Learn More about Our Life and Career Coaching Programs, Courses and Resources, visit: www.stephaniemahaliafletcher.com

---

Connect with me across various platforms for ongoing resources, inspiration, and community support.

YouTube Channel:

My Career, My Calling @mycareermycalling2868

https://www.youtube.com/channel/UCTlC9i-1jZ9FL3GfSCoBjyw

Get regular access to exclusive content focused on empowerment and growth.

- **Inspirational Content:** Webinars, workshops, and podcasts dedicated to **career empowerment** and **personal and professional development.**
- **Find It Here:** Search for **My Career, My Calling**

In-Depth Blogs

Dive deeper into strategic insights on professional growth.

- **Topics:** Various career and professional development-related topics, including leadership, mindset shifts, and navigating transitions.
- **Read Here: https://home.stephaniemahaliafletcher.com/blog**

Follow and Connect on Social Media

Join the conversation and connect with a community of professionals focused on living a vision-driven life.

Platform	Handle / Name
LinkedIn	**Dr. Stephanie Fletcher-Lartey**
Instagram	**drsteph_transformationcoach**
Facebook	**Fb.me/drstephtransformationcoach**

Other Creative Outputs by Dr. Stephanie Fletcher-Lartey

Books

- **Availability:** My books are available on **all major eBook platforms** and through **major distributors**.

Music

- **Platforms:** You can listen to my recorded songs on **Spotify, Apple Music,** and all other music streaming platforms.

APPENDICES

Appendix 1: Career Dream Blueprint: A Worksheet

This worksheet is designed to help you delve into your aspirations, values, and professional goals. Engage with each section thoughtfully, providing as much detail as possible to create a clear road map for your fulfilling career journey.

Section 1: Laying the Foundation: Purpose, Passions, and Core Values

To begin building a truly fulfilling professional life, it's essential to understand yourself at a fundamental level. This section will guide you in exploring your core motivations, talents, and ethical principles, which are the bedrock of a vision-driven career.

1a. What is Your Purpose?

Your purpose is the fundamental reason you exist—the unique contribution you were meant to make to the world. It provides direction and meaning, transforming work into a calling.

Reflection Prompts:

1. What is the fundamental reason you exist, or the unique contribution you believe you are meant to make to the world?
2. Reflect on the "why" behind your work. What deep-seated motivation fuels your actions and provides a sense of fulfilment?
3. Consider the questions that help uncover your "why":
    - Are you driven by a **passion for your work**?
    - Do you desire to make a **significant impact on society**?
    - Do you want to **use your unique talents and skills**?
    - Do you seek **autonomy and control over your work**?
    - Are you driven by **continuous learning and growth**?
4. Based on these, what specific "why" resonates most deeply with you?
5. Think about Alex, the software engineer who found purpose by using technology to connect food banks with restaurants. Does this example, or a similar one from your own life or observation, resonate with you in how you might find purpose in your work? Explain.

1b. What are Your Passions?

Passion is the energy that excites and motivates you. Aligning your career with your passion ensures work is a source of joy and fulfilment.

Reflection Prompts:

1. What activities or subjects truly excite and energise you, both inside and outside of work?
2. What would you do even if you weren't getting paid for it? (e.g., hobbies, books you read, activities you pursue in your free time)
3. How can you incorporate these passions into your professional life to make your work a source of genuine enjoyment and meaning?
4. Denis Diderot stated, "Only passions, great passions, can elevate the soul to great things". How does this quote inspire or apply to your aspirations for your career and the impact you wish to make?

1c. What are Your Core Values?

Your core values are the fundamental principles that guide your decisions and behaviour, acting as a moral compass. They are your non-negotiable standards for how you interact with the world and form the foundation of your character and integrity.

Action Steps & Reflection:

1. **Select Words:** Begin by selecting 3-5 words that naturally represent who you are, rather than aspirational qualities you wish to possess.
2. **Define Each Word:** Briefly define each word to understand its meaning and how you express it in your life.
    - (Word 1): Definition & Expression:
    -
    -
    -
    - (Word 2): Definition & Expression:
    -
    -
    -
    - (Word 3): Definition & Expression:
    -
    -
    -
    - (Word 4): Definition & Expression:
    -
    -
    -
    - (Word 5): Definition & Expression:
    -
    -
    -

3. **Narrow Down (if needed):** From your list, identify the **most essential, non-negotiable values**. These are the values that, if absent, would cause a noticeable shift in your being to those closest to you.
    - My Top 3-5 Core Values:
        ◦
        ◦
        ◦
        ◦
        ◦

4. **Seek Feedback:** Consider asking close friends or family to describe your presence using 3-5 words to further solidify your understanding of your core nature and values. Write down their feedback:
    - Feedback from Others:
        ◦
        ◦
        ◦
        ◦
        ◦

5. How do your core values act as a filtering system for your "yeses" and "no's" in both business and life? How would they guide your career decisions?

Section 2: Envisioning Your Ideal Future

Envisioning your ideal future is a creative process of connecting with your deepest motivations, serving as a guiding star for your aspirations. Allow your imagination to soar and visualise, in vivid detail, what you would love across various areas of your life.

Preparation Steps:

1. **Set the Atmosphere:** Find a quiet, private place where you won't be distracted. Relax, reflect, and connect with your inner voice.
2. **Practise Gratitude:** Before looking forward, take a moment to appreciate your current life and career experiences, skills, and relationships.

Visualisation Exercise:

Remaining in this calm, quiet, reflective atmosphere, begin to jot down all thoughts that come to mind about what your ideal career looks like. Even if the thoughts seem unrealistic, write them down, and for now, "set the how aside" to dream as expansively as possible.

Area of Life	What would your ideal future look like in these areas? (Be clear and detailed)
Health & Well-Being	
Love & Relationships	
Career/Business	
Financial Freedom & Personal Autonomy	

Reflective Visualisation Prompts:

1. **Explore Your Passions:** What activities or subjects truly excite and energise you in your free time? How could these be more central to your life?
2. **Visualise Your Ideal Work Environment:** Close your eyes and imagine the perfect work setting. What does it look like? Consider the pace, interaction style, autonomy, and company culture.
3. **Consider the Impact on Your Personal Life:** How will your ideal future support your well-being, relationships, and free time? How will you ensure a healthy work-life balance?

Action Step: Create a Vision Board Create a vision board using images, quotes, and symbols to visually represent your ideal life and career. This tangible representation will serve as a daily reminder of your goals and aspirations.

134 — CHAPTER 15: BUILDING YOUR BUSINESS:

Attach a picture or description of your vision board here:

Section 3: Envisioning Your Ideal Career and Work

This section focuses on specifically envisioning your ideal career—your dream vocation or creative expression. It's about finding profound fulfilment, purpose, and making a meaningful impact, aligned with your passions and values.

Reflection Prompts:

- What is the dream you have for your career—your ideal vocation or creative expression?
-
-
-

- Visualise your life three years from now if you were living that dream:

    - What are you doing?
    -
    -
    -

    - Who are you doing it with?
    -
    -
    -

    - What are you creating?
    -
    -
    -

    - What impact or difference are you making?
    -
    -
    -

- **Understanding Your "Why" in Career Progression:** Your "why" is the deep-seated motivation that fuels your actions and provides a sense of fulfilment. Reflect on the following questions to uncover your "why":
    - Are you driven by a **passion for your work**? Explain:
    -
    - Do you desire to make a **significant impact on society**? Explain:
    -
    - Do you want to **use your unique talents and skills**? Explain:
    -
    - Do you seek **autonomy and control over your work**? Explain:
    -

- Are you driven by **continuous learning and growth**? Explain:
-
- Summarise your core career "why":

Section 4: My Overall Career Dream

Documenting your vision is a crucial step in transforming it from a fleeting thought into a tangible goal. This section helps solidify your career dream and outlines how to engage with it regularly.

Writing Your Career Dream:

1. Start with the affirmation: **"I am grateful and happy that I am ____"** in these areas of my life. Do not censor yourself; write freely and allow your creativity to flow, dreaming boldly.

Engaging with Your Vision Regularly:

To truly bring your vision into reality, it's essential to engage with it consistently.

1. **Read it Aloud:** Commit to reading your career dream aloud to yourself daily or regularly. When will you do this?
    - Frequency/Time:
    -
    -

2. **Create an Audio or Video Recording (Optional):** If you create one, when and where will you listen to it?
    - When/Where:
    -
    -

3. **Check In with Your Vision Board:** Make it a habit to look at your vision board every day. When will this happen?
    - Frequency/Time:
    -
    -

4. **Carry a Wallet-Sized Version (Optional):** If you create a portable version, how will you use it as a constant companion?
    - Will you use it?
    -
    -

By making a habit of engaging with your vision, you are actively programming your mind to recognise opportunities and take the necessary actions to achieve your career dream. This consistent interaction keeps your goals top of mind and reinforces your commitment to the path you've chosen.

Appendix 2: The Growth & Resilience Toolkit

This toolkit is designed to be a hands-on guide for overcoming the mental roadblocks that may be holding you back in your career. By working through these exercises, you will learn to reframe limiting beliefs, confront your fears, and extract powerful lessons from past experiences. Refer to Chapters 2, 3 &4.

Part 1: Identifying & Reframing Limiting Beliefs (The 7 D's)

This section helps you pinpoint the subconscious patterns that might be sabotaging your progress. The 7 D's framework from Chapter 2 gives us a language to identify these patterns.

Exercise: Read through the 7 D's framework (Dissuasion, Delay/Distraction, DEFCON 1, Disdain, Deficiency, Disqualification, Displacement). Which of these resonate most with you? Write down one or two specific examples for each "D" that you have experienced in your career.

Identify Your "D's":

1. **Dissuasion:**
    - Example:
    - Example:
2. **Delay/Distraction:**
    - Example:
    - Example:
3. **DEFCON 1:**
    - Example:
    - Example:
4. **Disdain:**
    - Example:
    - Example:
5. **Deficiency:**
    - Example:
    - Example:
6. **Disqualification:**
    - Example:
    - Example:
7. **Displacement:**
    - Example:

- Example:

Reframing with "**Up until now**...":

Now, use the "Up until now..." statement to challenge and reframe these beliefs. For each of your identified "D's," complete the following sentence.

Up until now, I have believed that [old belief], but from this point forward, I choose to believe that [new, empowering belief].

- **Reframing for [D's you listed]:**
    - Up until now, I have believed... but from this point forward, I choose to believe...
    - Up until now, I have believed... but from this point forward, I choose to believe...

Part 2: Conquering Your Career Fears

Now that you've addressed your limiting beliefs, let's confront the specific fears that may be holding you back. This section helps you move from paralysis to action by creating a concrete plan.

Exercise: List your top three fears related to your career or professional goals. Be specific.

1. Fear: _____
2. Fear: _____
3. Fear: _____

Analyse the Impact: For each fear, answer these questions:

- How has this fear affected my career or professional choices?
- What's the worst-case scenario if this fear comes true?
- What's the best-case scenario if I face this fear?

Brainstorm & Plan: For each fear, brainstorm three concrete, actionable steps you can take to address or minimise it. These actions should be specific and measurable.

Fear #	Fear	Action 1	Action 2	Action 3
#1	[Your fear]			
#2	[Your fear]			
#3	[Your fear]			

Part 3: Reflecting on Past Failures

Our biggest setbacks can be our greatest teachers. This section provides a structured way to reflect on past failures, extract valuable lessons, and apply them for future success.

Exercise: Think of a significant professional failure or setback you've experienced. Briefly describe the situation and the outcome.

Description of Failure:

Analyse What Happened:

- What was within my control in this situation?
- What was outside of my control?
- What role did my mindset or beliefs play in this outcome?

Identify the Lessons:

What are the three most important lessons you learned from this experience? Think about skills, knowledge, or self-awareness.

1. Lesson 1:
2. Lesson 2:
3. Lesson 3:

Create a Forward-Looking Plan:

How will you apply these lessons to a current or future goal? Be specific about the action you'll take.

My Plan:

- To apply Lesson 1, I will...

- To apply Lesson 2, I will...

- To apply Lesson 3, I will...

Appendix 3: Skills Development & Growth Plan

This toolkit is designed to help you take a proactive and strategic approach to your professional development. Use it to inventory your current skills, identify where you need to grow, and create a concrete action plan to achieve your goals. Refer to Chapters 8 & 9.

CAREER SELF-ASSESSMENT

This tool is designed to help you systematically assess your skills, passions, and personality, providing a solid foundation for your career action plan. Work through each section thoughtfully, providing as much detail as possible.

Part 1: Skills & Strengths Inventory

This section helps you identify your core skills, including your "Zone of Genius" and "Zone of Excellence." Be honest in your self-evaluation.

A. Core Skill Set ("Zone of Genius")

Based on the 10 core skill sets, which ones feel most natural and effortless to you?

List your top 2-3 core skill sets. For each, provide a specific example of when you used it successfully.

Core Skill Set	Example of Use
1.	
2.	
3.	

B. Skill Assessment Table

This tool will help you complete a thorough self-assessment of your skills. List your specific skills and categorise them as Technical, Interpersonal, or Transferable. Rate your current proficiency and identify areas you want to develop.

Evaluate your proficiency in technical, interpersonal, and transferable skills. Rate your strength on a scale of 1-10 (1 = Novice, 10 = Expert).

142 — CHAPTER 15: BUILDING YOUR BUSINESS:

Skill Category	Specific Skill	Strength Level (1-10)	Areas for Improvement / Development Plan
Technical	(e.g., Python, Adobe Photoshop, CRM Software)		
Interpersonal	(e.g., Public Speaking, Team Leadership, Conflict Resolution)		
Transferable	(e.g., Problem-Solving, Critical Thinking, Time Management)		

Part 2: Personality Insights & Work Style

This section helps you understand the type of environment where you will thrive.

A. Ideal Work Environment

- **Pace:** (e.g., Fast-paced, Slower & Deliberate)
- **Interaction:** (e.g., Collaborative Teams, Independent Work)
- **Autonomy:** (e.g., High Autonomy, Clear Structure & Guidance)
- **Dress Code:** (e.g., Formal, Casual)
- **Company Culture:** (e.g., Innovative, Traditional, Socially-Driven)

B. Energy & Work Style

- Are you an **introvert** (energised by quiet, solo time) or an **extrovert** (energised by social interaction)?
- Are you a "morning person" or "night owl"?
- Do you prefer to focus on a few tasks at a time or enjoy multitasking?

C. Insights from Formal Assessments

If you have taken a formal personality or strengths test (e.g., Myers-Briggs, VIA Survey, Holland Code), what were the key takeaways? How do these insights align with the rest of your assessment

- **Holland Code Assessment (RIASEC)**

The Holland Code assessment, available online, helps you align your interests with potential career paths. It categorises individuals and jobs into six types: Realistic, Investigative, Artistic, Social, Enterprising, and Conventional (RIASEC).

You can find various free versions of this assessment online to help you review your results in a coaching session.

- **VIA Survey of Character Strengths**

The VIA Survey is a scientifically validated tool that helps you uncover your top character strengths. Understanding these strengths can provide profound self-awareness, allowing you to align your career with what you do best and what you find most fulfilling. You can access the survey for free online.

- **Other Assessments**

Dr Stephanie Fletcher-Lartey has development various digital Assessment tools that can be undertaken as a companion to this book. Contact her for access - visit www.stephaniemahaliafletcher.com

Summary & Action Steps

Review all three sections of your assessment. Look for patterns and connections. How do your skills, passions, and personality align to suggest a specific career path or area of focus? Write a short summary of your findings and list your top three career-related insights.

Part 3: SWOT Analysis Table

A SWOT analysis is a powerful strategic planning tool that helps you identify your internal Strengths and Weaknesses, as well as external Opportunities and Threats related to your career. Use this table to complete the analysis.

	Internal	External
Positive	**Strengths** (What are your unique skills, knowledge, and assets?)	**Opportunities** (What external trends, roles, or markets can you leverage?)

	Weaknesses	Threats
Negative	(What areas do you need to improve? What skills are you lacking?)	(What external factors could hinder your career goals? e.g., market trends, competition)

Personal SWOT Analysis

	Internal	External
Positive	**Strengths** (What are your unique skills, knowledge, and assets?)	**Opportunities** (What external trends, roles, or markets can you leverage?)
Negative	**Weaknesses** (What areas do you need to improve? What skills are you lacking?)	**Threats** (What external factors could hinder your career goals? e.g., market trends, competition)

Part 4: Reflective Journaling Prompts

Use these prompts to engage in regular reflective journaling. This practice helps you process experiences and clarify your professional goals and interests.

- What went well in my workday/week? What made it successful?
- What challenges did I face, and how did I handle them? What could I do differently next time?
- What did I learn today that I didn't know yesterday?
- What tasks or projects did I find most engaging, and why?
- What values or interests were activated (or neglected) in my work this week?
- Looking ahead, what is one small step I can take tomorrow to move closer to my career vision?

Part 5: Career Contingency Plan

A backup plan is a proactive strategy to mitigate risks and adapt to unexpected events. Use this table to create a contingency plan for a major career goal.

Career Goal	Potential Risk	Impact	Contingency Plan	Timeline
Example: Get a promotion	The role is given to someone else.	High	Speak with my manager about another growth path and get a detailed timeline for the next opportunity.	2 months

Part 6: Seeking Feedback Prompts

Actively seeking feedback is crucial for growth. Use these prompts with a trusted colleague or mentor to get specific, actionable feedback.

- "What is one thing I am doing well that I should continue to do?"
- "What is one thing I could improve upon to be more effective in my role?"
- "What skill or area of knowledge do you think would be most beneficial for me to develop for my long-term career goals?"
- "In your experience, what is the biggest mistake you see people in my role making, and how can I avoid it?"

"What communication assessment tools would you recommend for me to get objective feedback on my communication style?"

Part 7: Map Your Transferable Skills

7.1: Consolidated Transferable Skills Checklist

Transferable skills are the foundation of a successful career, especially in a rapidly changing work environment. Use the checklist below to assess your proficiency in a variety of key areas.

Instructions: Identify each skill you possess. Use the table to note your proficiency level (e.g., Beginner, Intermediate, Proficient) and provide specific examples of how you've used the skill.

Core Transferable Skills

Skill	Proficiency Level	Examples of Usage
Communication & Interpersonal Skills		
Active Listening		
Public Speaking & Presentation		
Written Communication		
Negotiation		
Empathy & Emotional Intelligence		
Conflict Resolution		
Networking		
Problem-Solving & Critical Thinking		
Analytical Skills		
Research & Data Gathering		
Problem Identification		
Logical Reasoning		
Creative Problem-Solving		
Organisational & Planning Skills		
Time Management		
Project Management		
Attention to Detail		
Strategic Planning		
Delegation		
Leadership & Teamwork		
Mentoring & Coaching		

Collaboration		
Giving & Receiving Feedback		
Adaptability		
Resilience		
Decision-Making		

AI-Augmented Skills

Instructions: This section focuses on skills that are enhanced by or necessary for working with AI and new technologies.

Skill	Proficiency Level	Examples of Usage
AI Literacy		
Prompt Engineering		
Data Analysis & Interpretation		
Digital Collaboration		
Information Curation		
Cybersecurity Awareness		

7.2: Enhanced Skills Gap Analysis & Action Plan

Now that you've identified your strengths, let's create a detailed plan to close any skills gaps. This five-step process will turn your aspirations into actionable steps.

Step 1: Define Your Goal

What specific professional goal are you working toward? (e.g., "Become a Senior Marketing Manager," "Launch my own consulting business," "Transition into a data science role.")

My Goal(s): ....

Step 2: List Required Skills

Based on your goal, what skills are absolutely essential for success? Be specific and refer to job descriptions or industry standards.

Required Skills: ....

Step 3: Identify Your Gap

Compare your checklist from Part 1 with the skills you listed in Step 2. Where are the gaps? What skills do you need to develop or improve?

My Skills Gaps: ....

Step 4: Create a Skills Development Strategy

Use the table below to create a detailed plan for closing your skills gaps.

Skill Gap	Development Strategy (Action)	Timeline
[e.g., Public Speaking]	[e.g., Enrol in Toastmasters]	[e.g., By the end of Quarter 3]
[e.g., Data Analysis]	[e.g., Complete the "Python for Data Science" course on Coursera]	[e.g., Within the next 3 months]

Step 5: Establish a Timeline

Include in your skills development strategy a concrete timeline for your action plan. Assign deadlines to each learning method to hold yourself accountable.

Appendix 4: Personal Brand Statement Worksheet

A powerful personal brand statement is a single sentence that concisely communicates your value and expertise. Use the prompts below to help you craft yours. Refer to Chapter 9.

Instructions: Answer each question, then combine your answers to create a single statement.

Who are you?

- What is your professional role, expertise, or core skill?

What do you do?

- What is the primary action or function you perform?

Who do you help?

- Who is your target audience or client?

What problem do you solve?

- What specific value or benefit do you provide?

Putting it all together

Combine your answers to form a single, powerful statement.

My Brand Statement:

Example: I am a creative content strategist who helps purpose-driven businesses tell compelling stories to connect with their audience and drive meaningful engagement.

Appendix 5: Résumé & Cover Letter Checklist

An effective résumé and cover letter are not one-size-fits-all. They should be tailored to each specific job application. Use this checklist to ensure your documents are perfectly aligned with the role you want. Refer to Chapter 9.

Checkbox	Task	Notes & Actions
[ ]	**Analyse the Job Description**	Read the description carefully and highlight the keywords, required skills, and responsibilities. [e.g., Highlight "project management," "client communication," and "data analysis."]
[ ]	**Incorporate Keywords**	Weave the language from the job description directly into your résumé's summary, experience section, and skills list. [e.g., Instead of "managed projects," write "Led agile projects from conception to completion."]
[ ]	**Highlight Relevant Transferable Skills**	Refer to the skills you identified in the previous toolkit and prominently feature those most relevant to the role. [e.g., If the job requires "leadership," highlight a time you mentored a junior colleague.]
[ ]	**Quantify Accomplishments**	Instead of just listing duties, use numbers, percentages, and metrics to show the impact of your work. [e.g., "Increased sales by 15% in Q2" instead of "Worked in sales."]
[ ]	**Customise the Cover Letter**	Write a unique cover letter for this specific company, explaining why you are passionate about their mission and how your skills can help them achieve their goals. [e.g., "I'm particularly drawn to [Company Name]'s mission because..." or "I admire your company's approach to..."]
[ ]	**Check for Consistency**	Ensure your résumé and cover letter tell a consistent story and reflect your personal brand statement.

Appendix 6: LinkedIn Profile Optimising Checklist

Your LinkedIn profile is your digital handshake. Use this checklist to optimise it for visibility, credibility, and strategic career positioning. Refer to Chapter 9.

Checkbox	Task	Notes & Actions
[ ]	**Professional Photo & Background**	Use a clear, high-quality head shot and a background image that reflects your industry or personal brand.
[ ]	**Compelling Headline**	Instead of just a job title, use keywords to describe the value you provide. (e.g., "Helping Businesses Grow with Data-Driven Marketing").
[ ]	**Personalised "About" Section**	Tell your professional story in your own voice, using a narrative that highlights your key skills and accomplishments.
[ ]	**Add and Endorse Skills**	Ensure your profile lists the core and AI-augmented skills you have and get endorsements from colleagues.
[ ]	**Request Recommendations**	Ask former managers, clients, or colleagues to write a brief recommendation.
[ ]	**Showcase Projects & Certifications**	Add relevant projects, certifications, and volunteer experience to demonstrate your expertise.
[ ]	**Engage with Content**	Like, share, and comment on industry-related articles and posts to increase your visibility.

Appendix 7: Comprehensive Career Action Plan

This tool is your personal road map, transforming your career aspirations into actionable steps and ensuring you continuously monitor and adjust your path toward fulfilling professional growth. Engage with each section thoughtfully to create a living document that guides your success. Refer to Chapters 10-11.

Section 1: Background and Foundation

This section summarises your initial self-discovery and strategic planning, serving as a vital reference point for your action plan.

1. **Self-Assessment Summary (Reflect on insights from Chapter 6):**

   - **Core Strengths & Zone of Genius:** Briefly summarise your top 2-3 core skill sets that feel most natural and effortless.
   - **Key Skills (Technical, Interpersonal, Transferable):** List your most important skills and your general proficiency level.
   - **Passions & Interests:** What genuinely excites and energises you? What problems do you love to solve?
   - **Core Values:** List your top 3-5 non-negotiable values that guide your decisions and behaviour.
   - **Personality Insights & Ideal Work Environment:** Describe your preferred work pace, interaction style, autonomy, and company culture.

2. **Overall Career Dream/Long-Term Vision (Reflect on insights from Chapter 1):**

   - What is your ultimate dream for your career? What impact do you want to make?

3. **Career Path Research Summary (Reflect on insights from Chapter 7):**

   - List potential job titles, industries, or companies that align with your vision, skills, interests, and values.
   - Key insights about these roles (e.g., required qualifications, market trends).

4. **Skills Analysis Summary (Reflect on insights from Chapters 8 & 9):**

- Key Skills to Develop (Identified Gaps): List the specific skills you need to acquire or improve to reach your goals.
- Key Transferable Skills to Leverage: How will you utilise your existing transferable skills to your advantage?

Section 2: Comprehensive Career Action Plan

(Reflect on insights from Chapters 7-10)

This is the core of your document, translating your vision and research into a practical, step-by-step plan.

Overall Career Goal (Your main aim for this plan):

_____
_____
_____
_____
_____
_____
_____
_____
_____
_____
_____
_____
___

Comprehensive Career Action Plan Template

Sub-goal / Objective (SMART)	Action Steps (Tasks I need to do)	Responsibility	Start Date	Deadline	Resources Needed	Tracking Method (Measures Progress)	Status (Not Started, In Progress, Completed)	Notes
Example: Skill Gap: Learn Staff Supervision (SMART: Enrol in and complete staff supervision training by Aug 31, 2024, to prepare for Office Manager role)	1. Enrol in staff supervision training program	Me	July 2024	Aug 31, 2024	Online training platform, training fees	Course completion	Not Started	Look for flexible options.
	2. Complete training program modules	Me	Sep 1, 2024	Sep 30, 2024	Training materials, online access	100% completion of modules	In Progress	Review weekly.

	3. Seek opportunities to supervise junior staff	Me	Oct 1, 2024	Ongoing	Internal team, senior manager support	Successfully leading at least one small project		Talk to my manager.
[Your Sub-goal/ Objective 1]	1.							
	2.							
	3.							
[Your Sub-goal/ Objective 2]	1.							
	2.							
	3.							
[Your Sub-goal/ Objective 3]	1.							
	2.							
	3.							

Section 3: Monitoring and Adjustment Log
(Reflect on insights from Chapter 11):

Your career plan is a **living document** that requires consistent attention and adaptability. This section outlines how you will continuously monitor your progress and make necessary adjustments.

1. Review Schedule:

- Frequency of Formal Reviews: (e.g., Monthly, Quarterly, Annually).
- Specific Dates/Periods for Reviews:
    - Q1 Review: _____
    - Q2 Review: _____
    - Q3 Review: _____
    - Q4 Review: _____

2. Progress Log (Document your achievements, challenges, and lessons learned):

Review Date	Achievements (What went well?)	Challenges Faced (What were the obstacles?)	Lessons Learned (What did you discover?)	Feedback Received (From whom, what was it?)

3. Plan Updates (Modifications to goals, timelines, or action steps):

Date of Update	Area Updated (e.g., Goal, Action Step, Timeline)	Original Plan	New/Revised Plan	Reason for Adjustment

4. Accountability and Support System (Reflect on insights from Chapter 12:

- Accountability Partner/Group: Who will help keep you on track? (e.g., mentor, friend, mastermind group).
- How you will engage with them: (e.g., weekly check-ins, monthly meetings).

This comprehensive template is designed to centralise your career planning efforts, providing a clear and adaptable framework to manifest your dream career. Remember to continuously engage with it, embrace continuous learning, and leverage your professional relationships to sustain your momentum.

Appendix 8: Continuous Learning and Relationships

This plan is a strategic tool designed to help you proactively manage your professional growth and expand your network. Use this template to create a clear, actionable road map for your career development. Refer to Chapter 12.

Continuous Learning and Professional Networking Plan

Name: _____ Date: _____

Review Date: _____

1. Skills Assessment

Current Skills:
_____
_____
_____

Areas for Improvement:
_____
_____

2. Objectives

Short-Term Goals (upcoming year):
_____
_____

Long-Term Goals (next 3–5 years):
_____
_____
_____
_____

3. Learning Opportunities

Courses/Certifications:
_____
_____

Workshops/Seminars:
_____
_____

Mentoring Opportunities:
_____
_____

Online Learning Platforms:
_____
_____

4. Networking Strategies

Target Individuals/Groups:
_____
_____

Monthly Networking Goals:
_____

Follow-Up Plan:
_____

5. Action Plan

Timeline:

_____
_____
_____
_____
_____
_____
_____
_____
_____
_____

Resources Needed:

_____
_____
_____
_____
_____

6. Review & Feedback

Progress Notes:

_____
_____
_____
_____
_____

Adjustments:

_____
_____
_____
_____
_____
_____
_____
_____
_____
_____
_____

Bibliography

Books and Academic Works

- Abur, W. (2022). Migration and Settlement of African People in Australia. In I. Muenstermann (Ed.), *The Changing Tide of Immigration and Emigration During the Last Three Centuries*. IntechOpen.
- Covey, S. R. (1989). *The 7 habits of highly effective people: Restoring the character ethic*. Simon & Schuster.
- Dweck, C. S. (2006). *Mindset: The new psychology of success*. Random House.
- Fisher, H. (2013). *The Plight of African Migrants in Australia: Social and Economic Consequences*.
- Gandhi, M. (2019). *The wisdom of Gandhi*. Arcturus Publishing.
- Holland, J. L. (1997). *Making vocational choices: A theory of vocational personalities and work environments*. Psychological Assessment Resources.
- Kabat-Zinn, J. (1994). *Wherever you go, there you are: Mindfulness meditation in everyday life*. Hyperion.
- Mandino, O. (1968). *The greatest salesman in the world*. Frederick Fell, Inc.
- Munroe, M. (2018). *The principles and power of vision*. Whitaker House.
- Nietzsche, F. (2008). *Twilight of the idols*. (Original work published 1888).
- Robinson, K., Afrouz, R., & Dunwoodie, E. (2025). *African Migrant Skills Utilisation in Australian Employment: A Longitudinal Study*.
- Stahl, A. (2021). *You turn: Get unstuck, discover your direction, and design your dream career*. Grand Central Publishing.
- The Motivation Lounge. (2023, March 16). *25 People Who Over Came Adversity To Become Successful*. Retrieved September 10, 2025, from https://themotivationlounge.com/25-people-who-over-adversity-to-become-successful/
- Trimm, C. (2017). *Hello tomorrow: The creative power of your mind*. Charisma House.
- Vasil, L. (2023). *Economic Precarity and the Autonomy of Migrant Women*.

Other Formats

- African Australian Advocacy Centre (AAAC). (2025). *We Belong Here Framework for Human Rights and Equity*. Submission to the Senate Standing Committee on Legal and Constitutional Affairs.
- Australian Parliament. (2011). *Chapter 8 Africans in Australia*. Address in Reply.
- Covey, S. R. (2004). *The 8th habit: From effectiveness to greatness*. Simon and Schuster.
- D'avella, M. (2019, September 3). *The two days rule for consistency*. [Video]. YouTube. https://youtu.be/bfL-HTLQZ5nc
- Diderot, D. (1746). *Pensées philosophiques*. (Original work published 1746)
- Edwards, E. (2025). *Transferable Skills in the AI Era: How Your Expertise Remains Valuable*. LinkedIn. Retrieved September 10, 2025, from https://www.linkedin.com/pulse/transferable-skills-ai-era-how-your-expertise-remains-edwards-dv4gf
- Fletcher-Lartey, S. (Host). (2019). *My Career, My Calling -Special Episode: Job Readiness Seminar Part 1* [Video podcast transcript]. My Career, My Calling. Fletcher-Lartey, S. (Host). (2019). *My Career, My Calling Episode 3 (Preparing for Work Pt 2) - with guest Emmanuel Adjei* [Video podcast transcript]. My Career, My Calling. Fletcher-Lartey, S. (Host). (2019). *My Career, My Calling Special Episode Part 2B - Job Readiness Seminar - Aug 6, 2019* [Video podcast transcript]. My Career, My Calling. Fletcher-Lartey, S. (Host). (2019). *My Career My Calling Intro (Episode1 - Part 1) with Stephanie Fletcher-Lartey* [Video podcast transcript]. My Career, My Calling. Fletcher-Lartey, S. (Host). (2019). *Transcript - Julia Mapenzi: My Career, My Calling Episode 4 (Preparing for Work Pt 3) - with guest Julia Mapenzi* [Video podcast transcript]. My Career, My Calling.
- Foy, T. S. (2015). *Dream it. Pin it. Live it.: Make Vision Boards Work for You*. [PDF]. Retrieved from https://www.terri.com/wp-content/uploads/sites/26/2019/04/Dream-It-WB-Ebook.pdf

- Hugo, G. (2009). *Migration between Africa and Australia: a demographic perspective*. Background paper for African Australians: A review of human rights and social inclusion issues. Australian Human Rights Commission.
- ILO. (2024). *Global Employment Trends for Youth 2024*. International Labour Organisation.
- ILO. (2024). *World Employment and Social Outlook: May 2024 Update*. International Labour Organisation.
- Jackson, J. (2019). [Interview on career transition]. In S. Fletcher-Lartey (Host), *My Career, My Calling Episode 10 (Navigating Career Crossroads) - with Jane Jackson, Career Coach* [Video podcast transcript]. My Career, My Calling.
- Morrissey, M. (2022, December 21). *How Your Thoughts Determine Your Success with Mary Morrisey*. [Video]. The Achieve Your Goals Podcast with Hal Elrod. https://www.youtube.com/watch?v=g2ffUOtiRn8
- Morrissey, M. (2022, December 12). *3 ways to shift your paradigm and manifest your dreams*. Brave Thinking Institute. Retrieved September 10, 2025, from https://www.bravethinkinginstitute.com/blog/life-transformation/shift-your-paradigm
- Morrissey, M. (2018, February 5). *Defining paradigms: Facts vs. truth*. Brave Thinking Institute. Retrieved September 10, 2025, from https://www.bravethinkinginstitute.com/blog/life-transformation/define-paradigms-facts-vs-truth
- Morrissey, M. (2015). *The process of forming a paradigm*. HuffPost. Published online June 13, 2015. Retrieved September 10, 2025, from https://www.huffpost.com/entry/the-process-of-forming-a_b_7561150
- Morrissey, M. (2022, January 6). *Paradigms 101: Examples from real people in all walks of life*. Brave Thinking Institute. Retrieved September 10, 2025, from https://www.bravethinkinginstitute.com/blog/life-transformation/paradigms-101
- Munroe, M. (2022, July 2). *10 Keys For Personal Success || Dr. Myles Munroe*. [Video]. YouTube. https://www.youtube.com/watch?v=IxOdErVAsNM
- Proaction International. (2025). The Importance of Soft Skills and AI. Retrieved September 10, 2025, from https://blog.proactioninternational.com/en/importance-soft-skills-and-ai
- Proctor, B. (n.d.). [Accountability concept].
- Red Hat. (2025). *Thinking Big, Starting Small: Why Focused AI is Set to Win in 2025*. Retrieved September 10, 2025, from https://www.redhat.com/en/blog/thinking-big-starting-small-why-focused-ai-set-win-2025
- SAFETY4SEA. (2025). *Shaping the future: Critical thinking in the age of machines*. Retrieved September 10, 2025, from https://safety4sea.com/cm-shaping-the-future-critical-thinking-in-the-age-of-machines
- World Economic Forum. (2023). *The future of jobs report 2023*. World Economic Forum. https://www3.weforum.org/docs/WEF_Future_of_Jobs_2023.pdf
- YouTube. (2020, December 1). *Force yourself to get it done: Dr. Myles Munroe's key to success*. [Video]. YouTube. https://www.youtube.com/watch?v=sI9eYl_388w

Index

7
7 D's, 23

A
A Recap of Your Journey, 146
About the Author, iv
Accountability, 113
Accountability and Support System, 198
Acknowledging Discomfort with Your Current Situation, 21
Actionable Steps for Mindset Development, 138
Addressing Barriers at Individual and Organisational Levels, 36
AI-Augmented Skills, 187
Answering the Roar, 30
APPENDICES, 158

B
Beyond Boundaries, i
Bibliography, 202
Bridging the Gap, 64
Building Your Business, 140

C
Career Action Planning, 45, 147
Career Contingency Plan, 182
Career Dream Blueprint: A Worksheet, 159
Career planning, 47
Case Study: Administrative Assistant to Office Manager, 75
Common Fears and Their Impact on Career Growth, 22
Components of a Career Action Plan, 49
Comprehensive Career Action Plan Template, 194, 196
Career Self-Assessment, 174
Conducting a Self-Assessment, 56
Conquering Your Career Fears, 172
Consolidated Transferable Skills Checklist, 184
Contingency Planning, 58
Continuous improvement, 142
Continuous Learning Plan, 144

Core Transferable Skills, 184
Core Values, 13, 161
Create a Vision Board, 165
Creating a Comprehensive Career Action Plan, 99
Creating a Vision for Your Life, 11
Cultivating a Resilience Mindset, 39

D

Debunking Common Myths about Career Planning, 3
DEFCON 1, 24
Defense Readiness Condition 1, 25
Definition of Transferable Skills, 81
Designing a Dream for Your Career, 10
Designing the Dream, 15
Developing a Backup Plan, 59
Displacement, 24
Dissuasion, 24
Diversity Challenges, 36

E

Envisioning Your Ideal Career, 17
Envisioning Your Ideal Career and Work, 166
Envisioning Your Ideal Future, 164
Essential Skills for the Modern Entrepreneur, 141
Example Career Action Plan for Administrative Assistant, 106
External Barriers, 34

G

Gender and Diversity Barriers, 35
Gender Bias, 36
growth mindset, 41

H

Holland Code, 58
Holland Code Assessment (RIASEC), 177, 181
How the 7 Ds Manifest in Careers, 23

I

Identifying & Reframing Limiting Beliefs (The 7 D's), 170
Identifying Negative Mindsets and Self-Limiting Beliefs, 22
Identifying What Truly Matters to You, 15

Inclusivity, 36
Intentional Thinking for Accelerated Career Growth, 45
Internal Barriers, 34
Introduction, 1
Irresistible Offer, 143

K
Keeping Your Vision Alive, 18

L
Laying the Foundation: Purpose, Passions, and Core Values, 159
Leveraging Self-Belief, 138
Leveraging Transferable Skills, 81, 85
Leveraging Your Skills to Start Your Own Business, 136

M
Marketing Strategies, 143
Marketing Transferable Skills, 87
Monitoring and Adjusting Your Career Action Plan, 111
My Overall Career Dream, 168

N
Navigating Challenges and Embracing Change, ii
Navigating Your Career Journey with Clarity and Purpose, 1
Networking, 59
Networking Action Plan, 117

P
paradigms, 22
Part 2: Enhanced Skills Gap Analysis & Action Plan, 188
Passion & Interests Audit, 56
Passion: The Fuel for Your Career, 12
Paying Attention to Your Thoughts, 40
Personal SWOT Analysis, 179
Personality Insights, 57
Personality Insights & Work Style, 177
Preface, i
Progress Log, 198
Purpose, 159
Purpose: The "Why" Behind Your Work, 11

R
Racial Discrimination, 36
Reflecting on Past Failures, 173
Reflective Journaling, 58
Reflective Journaling Prompts, 181
Reflective Visualization Prompts, 164
Re-patterning Your Mindset: Shifting to a Proactive State, 26
Researching Career Options, 68
Resilience and Perseverance, 138
Risk Management Strategies, 58

S
Sales Process, 143
Seeking Feedback Prompts, 183
Self-Assessment Tools, 57
Self-limiting beliefs, 22
Self-Reflection and Skills Assessment, 143
Setting SMART Career Goals and Researching, 62
Skill Assessment Table, 175
Skill Diversification, 59
Skills & Strengths Inventory, 174
Skills Assessment, 53
Skills Development & Growth Plan, 174
skills gap analysis, 71
Skills Inventory Table, 179
Skillset and Toolset for Success, 140
SMART Goals, 62
Strategic planning, 141
Strategies for Building Your Network, 116
Strategies to Repattern Your Mindset, 31
Structured Approach to Goal Setting, 65
Success Stories, 37
Sustaining Momentum, 147
SWOT Analysis, 57, 179

T
The 10 Core Skill Sets, 55
The Action Plan, 103
The Entrepreneurial Mindset, 136
The Foundation, 146
The Foundation: From Grassroots to Global Health Impact, iv

The Growth & Resilience Toolkit, 170
The Mind-Body Connection, 28
The Mindset of a Proactive Professional, 120
The Multi-Talented Professional, v
The Power of Mastermind Groups and Partners, 122
The Power of Mindset, 39
The Power of Self-Reflection, ii
The Power of Vision and Intention, 137
The Results Formula, 40
The Role of Coaching and Mentoring, 74, 79
The Value of a Career Action Plan, 2
Transferable Skills in the Age of AI, 83

U
Understanding Barriers, 34
Understanding Career Planning, 47
Understanding Skills Gaps, 71
Understanding the Components of an Action Plan, 100
Understanding Your "Why" in Career Progression, 10

V
VIA Survey of Character Strengths, 177, 181
Visualisation Exercise, 164

W
What are Your Passions, 160
What This Resource Guide Provides, 7
Why You Need This Guide, 8
Writing Your Career Dream, 168

Y
Your Nervous System, 28
Your Path Forward, 148
Your Skills & Strengths Inventory, 56

Z
Zone of Excellence, 54
Zone of Genius, 54

www.ingramcontent.com/pod-product-compliance
Lightning Source LLC
Chambersburg PA
CBHW051157290426
44109CB00022B/2493